MIRROR ON

1930

ISBN: 9781675114735

INDEX

INDEX - 2

INDEX - 3

INDEX - 4

VISCOUNT WOLMER AND MAIL BAG ROBBERIES

DailyMirror

THE DAILY PICTURE PAPER WITH THE LARGEST NET SALE

No. 8,154   Registered at the G.P.O. as a Newspaper.   MONDAY, JANUARY 6, 1930   One Penny

WINSTON'S RIVAL

Mr. Snowden, in unconventional Ministerial headgear, leaving a preliminary session of the second Hague Conference that will hold its first ordinary sitting to-day. Important conversations have already taken place between delegates from different countries represented.

ROYAL BRIDE IN ROME

The Chapel Paolina in the Quirinal Palace at Rome, where the wedding of the Crown Prince of Italy and Princess Marie-Jose of Belgium (inset) will be celebrated. The Princess arrived at Rome yesterday and was met at a suburban station by her bridegroom, who travelled with her to the Central Station.

LORANG FOUND

Francis Lorang, missing chairman of Blue Bird Petrol Company, arrested at Montmartre, Paris, after a nine months' search in many countries. Extradition has been applied for.

STREET ATTACK

Miss Laura Woollard, aged eighteen, of Grantham-road, Manor Park, who was attacked at Forest Gate and entered a shop with a wound in her throat. A man is detained.

PILOT'S ESCAPE WHEN HIS 'PLANE HITS A TREE

Wreckage of an aeroplane which made a forced landing in the grounds of Wa'l Hall, Aldenham, Herts, and crashed into a tree. Mr. Reginald Brie, the pilot, suffered from shock.

MANY INSURANCE CLAIMS PAID: REGISTER NOW

£550
PICTURE
PUZZLE
PRIZE

DailyMirror

THE DAILY PICTURE PAPER WITH THE LARGEST NET SALE

No. 8,155   Registered at the G.P.O. as a Newspaper.   TUESDAY, JANUARY 7, 1930   One Penny

£100
CROSSWORD
PUZZLE

ITALY'S GREETINGS TO HER FUTURE QUEEN

The King of the Belgians at the tomb of the Unknown Soldier in Rome. The marriage of his daughter will take place to-morrow.

BATSMAN'S GREAT RECORD

Don Bradman, whose score of 452 not out for New South Wales against Queensland at Sydney yesterday set up a world's record. It is the highest individual score in first-class cricket. The previous best was Ponsford's 437.

The brilliant scene at the Rome Central Station as the carriage containing Princess Marie-Jose of Belgium and her fiancé, the Crown Prince of Italy, was moving off. The Roman population's welcome to their future Queen on her arrival from Brussels was almost delirious, and seldom has such a spectacle of pageantry been seen. All along the route the houses were gaily decorated. See also page 20.—(Agenzia Stefani and " Daily Mirror " photo-telephony.)

8

£1,000 ZIG-ZAG: LAST CHANCE TO SEND SOLUTIONS

GRAMOPHONE ARTICLE TO-DAY

DailyMirror

THE DAILY PICTURE PAPER WITH THE LARGEST NET SALE

SPECIAL EDITION

No. 8,157   Registered at the G.P.O. as a Newspaper.   THURSDAY, JANUARY 9, 1930   One Penny

THE CROWN PRINCE OF ITALY'S WEDDING

The Prince of Piedmont and Princess Marie-Jose, who were married in the Pauline Chapel of the Quirinal Palace at Rome yesterday.

Neapolitans attending the festivities in their picturesque traditional costumes.

A picture received last night by "Daily Mirror" photo-telephony of the royal party driving in front of St. Peter's after visiting the Pope. The Papal Swiss Guards in their splendid uniforms, which have not been altered since the Renaissance, are saluting.

There were five Kings, five Queens and representatives of many foreign nations present when the Heir to the Italian Crown and the only daughter of the King of the Belgians were married by Cardinal Maffi. See also page 24. (Agenzia Stefani.)

NEW SERIAL, "ONE WAY STREET," ON TUESDAY

RADIO GOSSIP TO-DAY

DailyMirror

THE DAILY PICTURE PAPER WITH THE LARGEST NET SALE

No. 8,158   Registered at the G.P.O. as a Newspaper.   FRIDAY, JANUARY 10, 1930   One Penny

LOMBARD THE BEST CITY GUIDE

PRINCE OPENS NATIONAL GALLERY ANNEXE

Prince George talking with Lady Chamberlain in the new Duveen Gallery which he opened at the National Gallery yesterday. Sir Joseph Duveen presented this annexe for pictures of the Venetian and Northern Italian schools. A special system of lighting has been adopted to avoid reflections on the glass protecting the canvases.

FOR NEW RECORD?

Miss Amy Johnson, the first British woman to obtain an Air Ministry licence as a ground engineer, is planning, it is stated, to attempt a record flight to Australia in a new machine, the details of which are secret.

PREMIER RECEIVES JAPANESE DELEGATES

Mr. Ramsay MacDonald with the Japanese delegates to the London Naval Conference during a private discussion which they had with him at 10, Downing-street last night. (X) Mr. Wakatsuki, former Japanese Premier.

O.P. CLUB'S LOSS

Mr. Carl Hentschel, who founded the O.P. Club forty-five years ago to foster the love of playgoing, died yesterday afternoon at the age of sixty-six. He was a former member of the City Corporation.

10

"ONE WAY STREET," BY ALEC WAUGH, TO-MORROW

FILM NOTES TO-DAY

Daily Mirror

THE DAILY PICTURE   PAPER WITH THE LARGEST NET SALE

No. 8,160   Registered at the G.P.O as a Newspaper.   MONDAY, JANUARY 13, 1930   One Penny

SPECIAL EDITION

BLIZZARD SWEEPS OVER GREAT BRITAIN

A postman delivering letters near Ribblehead, Yorkshire.

A ski-ing party setting out for a run at Glenshee, Perthshire.

Tobogganing exhilaration in Perthshire.

A shepherd driving in his flock near Hawes, North Yorkshire.

Competitors battling against the adverse weather during a cross-country run at Northolt, Middlesex.

Accidents and mishaps were caused during the week-end by gale and snow, which fell heavily in many parts of Great Britain. Frost made London road surfaces dangerous and several people were injured when an omnibus shot through a wall at Maida Vale. A fierce gale and dangerous seas were experienced in the Channel last night.

11

"ONE WAY STREET" BEGINS TO-DAY ON PAGE 15

£500 PICTURE PUZZLE WEEKLY

DailyMirror

THE DAILY PICTURE PAPER WITH THE LARGEST NET SALE

No. 8,161   Registered at the G.P.O. as a Newspaper.   TUESDAY, JANUARY 14, 1930   One Penny

£100 CROSSWORD PUZZLE

TERRIBLE ROAD RISKS RUN IN THE GALE

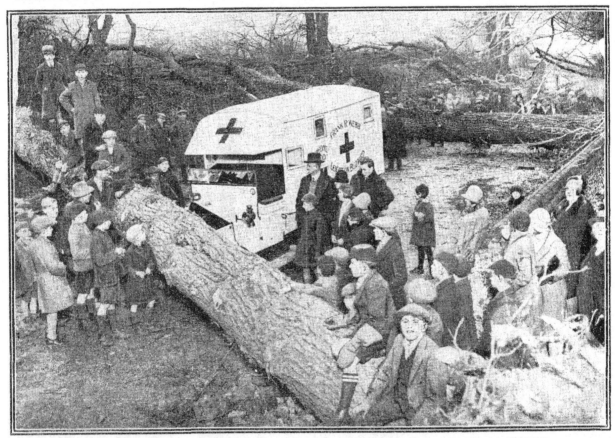

A tree fallen across an ambulance in Gadebridge Park, Herts, where a man was killed and a policeman injured. Another car was damaged near by.

A wrecked G.W.R. motor-bus at Farnham, Bucks. No one was hurt.

A bus which, when taking passengers to Hemel Hempstead, narrowly avoided disaster.

Many people were killed or injured and a yet larger number had remarkable escapes on the roads of Southern England during the worst hurricane of this winter, which has been so remarkable for gales. A motor-cyclist and a girl riding pillion dashed against an obstructing trunk and received fatal injuries at Rowfant, Sussex. Near Kenilworth there was another double fatality when a tree crashed on to a lorry and killed the driver and his mate. See also pages 12, 13 and 24.

DailyMirror

THE DAILY PICTURE   PAPER WITH THE LARGEST NET SALE

No. 8,163   Registered at the G.P.O. as a Newspaper.   THURSDAY, JANUARY 16, 1930   One Penny

BRITISH BATTLESHIP RUNS ON THE ROCKS

H.M.S. Ramillies, a battleship of 25,750 tons, which, while entering port yesterday, went ashore on Fort Santangelo rocks, in the middle of Grand Harbour at Valetta, Malta. | She became fast from her foremost gun turret to her bows and six tugs were sent to her assistance. These subsequently refloated her.

THE PRINCE'S YOUTHFUL PARTNER

FREE STATE'S FIRST PAPAL NUNCIO ARRIVES IN DUBLIN

Miss Pamela Delance Young, a twelve-year-old passenger on the Kenilworth Castle, with whom the Prince of Wales danced a fox-trot at a fancy dress ball on deck.

Monsignor Pascal Robinson (B), the first Papal Nuncio to the Irish Free State, with Dr. Byrne (A), Archbishop of Dublin, and President Cosgrave (C) at the Dun Laoghaire promenade after Dr. Robinson's arrival at Dublin. Yesterday he presented his credentials to the Governor-General, Mr. James McNeill.

FIRST TEST ARTICLE BY MACARTNEY TO-DAY

FREE HAMPERS WINNERS' NAMES

Daily Mirror

THE DAILY PICTURE PAPER WITH THE LARGEST NET SALE

SPECIAL EDITION

No. 8,165   Registered at the G.P.O. as a Newspaper.   SATURDAY, JANUARY 18, 1930   One Penny

U.S. NAVAL DELEGATES ARRIVE IN LONDON

The American delegation to the Naval Conference with British Ministers on arrival at Paddington yesterday. Left to right, Mr. C. F. Adams, United States Secretary for the Navy, Mr. A. V. Alexander, Mr. H. L. Stimson, United States Secretary of State, Mr. Arthur Henderson, General Dawes, Senator J. T. Robinson and Mr. Dwight Morrow.

Some of the typists who accompany the delegation. Also with the official party are Mrs. Stimson, Mrs. Adams, Mrs. Robinson, Mrs. Morrow and Miss Elizabeth Morrow. The Conference will be opened by the King at the House of Lords on Tuesday.—("Daily Mirror.")

MISS BRANSON MURDER TRIAL OPENS

Francois Pinet, aged twenty-five, in the dock at Aix-en-Provence Assizes yesterday, where his trial began. He is charged with the murder of Miss Olive Branson (inset), who was found dead near her villa at Les Baux in April last year.—(Picture wired from Marseilles.)

BOMBSHELL FOR MOTORISTS IN ROAD BILL

150 FREE HAMPERS WEEKLY

DailyMirror

THE DAILY PICTURE PAPER WITH THE LARGEST NET SALE

LOMBARD THE BEST CITY GUIDE

No. 8,174 Registered at the G.P.O. as a Newspaper. WEDNESDAY, JANUARY 29, 1930 One Penny

RESIGNATION OF SPANISH DICTATOR

King Alfonso in conversation with General Primo de Rivera, whose resignation he accepted.

General Berenguer, the new Premier.

The Dictator with Senorita N. Castillano. He broke off his engagement to her in 1928 because she was seen buying shares in the Stock Exchange.

Signor Anido, Minister of the Interior.

General Primo de Rivera, Premier and Dictator of Spain, has resigned after holding office since 1923. He had conferred with several Ministers, including Signor Anido, General Berenguer succeeds him. The new Premier was sentenced to six months' imprisonment in a fortress in 1924 for attending a banquet at which speeches were made attacking the Dictator, but was pardoned after three months. General Berenguer is the Chief of the King's Military Household.

GARAGE MURDER: DRAMATIC EVIDENCE

MOTOR ARTICLE TO-DAY

DailyMirror

THE DAILY PICTURE PAPER WITH THE LARGEST NET SALE

No. 8,175   Registered at the G.P.O. as a Newspaper.   THURSDAY, JANUARY 30, 1930   One Penny

£10,000 FREE INSURANCE

TUBE TO SOLVE A LONDON TRAVEL PROBLEM

Passengers leaving an Ilford train at Liverpool-street.

Eighteen such trains leave Ilford Station between seven and nine every morning.

District to be served by the proposed tube railway.

HER £20,000 FINE

Mrs. Frank Vane Storrs, a wealthy American society woman, who has been fined the sum of £20,000 in New York for smuggling jewellery which she had brought into the United States several years before.

A large crowd waiting at Liverpool-street for out-going trains. The congestion of traffic would be greatly relieved if a scheme for the construction of a new tube to Ilford—now being considered by the London and North Eastern Railway—should materialise. The Ministry of Transport and Mr. J. H. Thomas have taken part in negotiations.

HAIR-WAVING CLAIM

Miss Edith Clara Bowden, of Elgin-terrace, W., who, in the King's Bench Division yesterday sued a firm of hair-dressers for damages for injuries alleged to have been received during per-manent waving.

THE DAILY MIRROR, Thursday, February 6, 1930.

£10 PRIZE FOR BEST WEEKLY BUDGET: PAGE 4

DailyMirror

THE DAILY PICTURE PAPER WITH THE LARGEST NET SALE

No. 8,181   Registered at the G.P.O. as a Newspaper.   THURSDAY, FEBRUARY 6, 1930   One Penny

THE DUKE HONOURS BRITISH VICTORS OF THE AIR

The Duke of York (H) at the Royal Aero Club dinner held at the Savoy Hotel last night to celebrate the Schneider Trophy and other British air triumphs. Other guests are Lady Wakefield (A), Lady Bailey (B), the Duchess of Bedford (C), Mrs. Stainforth (D), Mrs. D'Arcy Greig (E), Mrs. Orlebar (F), Squadron-Leader Orlebar (G), Lieut.-Col. J. C. Moore-Brabazon (J), and Flight-Lieut. D'Arcy Greig (K), who was married last week. Flight-Lieut. Waghorn, Schneider Trophy winner, received a certificate.

The Duke of York handing Lady Bailey the Britannia Trophy for her flight alone to Capetown and back. The club's gold medal was presented to Captain C. D. Barnard and an illuminated address to the Duchess of Bedford for their flight to India and back.—("Daily Mirror" photographs.)

THE BEAUTY QUEEN OF EUROPE

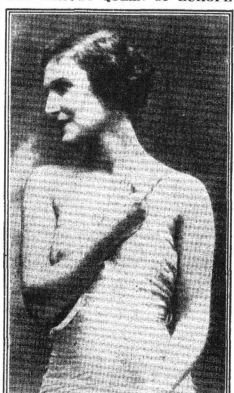

Mlle. Alice Diplarakou after she had been declared the winner of the beauty competition of Europe in Paris yesterday. Her election as "Miss Greece" at Athens was marked by a riot, members of the jury being roughly handled when their decision was given.—(By "Daily Mirror" photo-telephony from Paris last night.)

OXFORD COACHES RESIGN—DISPUTE WITH PRESIDENT

Dr. P. C. Mallam.   Major A. F. Wiggins.   Mr. A. S. Garton.   Mr. Alaistair Graham.

Dr. P. C. Mallam, Major A. F. Wiggins and Mr. A. S. Garton, coaches of the Oxford Boat Race crew, have resigned their positions following disagreement with Mr. Alaistair Graham, president of the Boat Club, regarding the composition of the crew. Mr. Graham has complete authority.

17

THE DAILY MIRROR, Monday, February 10, 1930.

PARIS AND THE LONG SKIRT: SEE PAGE 19

DailyMirror

THE DAILY PICTURE PAPER WITH THE LARGEST NET SALE

No. 8,184   Registered at the G.P.O as a Newspaper.   MONDAY, FEBRUARY 10, 1930   One Penny

RACEGOERS RUN RIOT AND WRECK COURSE

Chairs and ticket-boxes strewing the racecourse after extraordinary scenes of violence at a trotting meeting at Vincennes, near Paris, yesterday.

Railings uprooted by the frenzied mob.

A totalisator booth with windows broken and awnings pulled down.

Firemen fighting a conflagration started by a crowd of exasperated racegoers who rushed about the course doing all the damage they could following a race which was decided after a false start. The police, both mounted and on foot, were unable to check the rioting for a time. Extensive damage was done to the stewards' and the owners' quarters, the weighing room and other buildings. Several people were wounded and a number of arrests made.—("Daily Mirror" photo-telephony.)

THE DAILY MIRROR Wednesday, February 12, 1930

MORE PRIZES FOR WORKING GIRLS' BUDGETS

DailyMirror

THE DAILY PICTURE — PAPER WITH THE LARGEST NET SALE

No. 8,186 — Registered at the G.P.O. as a Newspaper. — WEDNESDAY, FEBRUARY 12, 1930 — One Penny

TENNIS STAR TO WED SHORTLY

Miss Evelyn Colyer, the English lawn tennis star and daughter of Sir Frank Colyer, is to be married to Mr. Hamish Munro (inset) in London next week. Mr. Munro is an Assam tea planter, and his fiancée will give up first-class tennis. They first met some five weeks ago in Switzerland.

ABOLISH SUBMARINES PLEA

One of the newest British submarines, which, with all undersea vessels, would be scrapped if Britain's point of view, explained by Mr. A. V. Alexander (inset), First Lord of the Admiralty, at the plenary session of the Naval Conference at St. James's Palace yesterday, were adopted by the other great Naval powers. America supported Britain, but France and Japan were in favour of retention.

WED AT 78

Mr. F. J. Hanbury, aged seventy-eight, well-known manufacturer, of East Grinstead, who has married Miss Mary Satow and left for Algeria yesterday for the honeymoon.

EX-ENEMY

Jafar Pasha, the Iraq Minister in London, who was captured by the Dorset Yeomanry at Agagia in 1916, has promised to attend their dinner at Weymouth on February 26.

WORK BEGUN ON BATHING PAVILION FOR HYDE PARK "LIDO"

Workmen by the side of the Serpentine in Hyde Park yesterday clearing the space allotted for a new bathing pavilion, which is expected to be ready next May. It is part of Mr. Lansbury's "Lido in London" scheme.

£500 PRIZE AND 150 FREE HAMPERS WEEKLY

FILM NOTES TO-DAY

DailyMirror

THE DAILY PICTURE PAPER WITH THE LARGEST NET SALE

£1,000 RACING CONTEST COUPON

No. 8,190   Registered at the G.P.O. as a Newspaper.   MONDAY, FEBRUARY 17, 1930   One Penny

AN ULTIMATUM

PEER PUSHING THE PRAM

Gandhi (right), the Indian agitator, who is expected to draft to-day an ultimatum to the Viceroy (Lord Irwin, left), as the first step in the "war of independence" on which the extremists are now embarking. An attack on the salt revenue is a likely first move.

THREE HURT IN COACH CRASH

Lord Gorell wheels a perambulator containing his baby daughter and son (who is beneath the hood) in Hyde Park yesterday during the spring-like sunshine which took so many people out of doors.

A wrecked telegraph pole near Sawtry, Huntingdonshire, into which a Newcastle-London motor-coach crashed after a skid. Right, the smashed coach. Three passengers of the ten who were in the coach were detained in hospital, and the others went home by train. The injured were from Middlesbrough and West Hartlepool.

20

VISCOUNT ROTHERMERE AND THE NEW PARTY

THEATRE NOTES TO-DAY

DailyMirror

THE DAILY PICTURE PAPER WITH THE LARGEST NET SALE

No. 8,192 Registered at the G.P.O. as a Newspaper. WEDNESDAY, FEBRUARY 19, 1930 One Penny

£1,000 RACING CONTEST COUPON

WRECKED LINER CAPTAIN'S HEROIC DEATH

The German liner Monte Cervantes, of 13,913 tons, which belonged to the Hamburg-South America Line, heels over with the captain on board.

Passengers wearing lifebelts grouped on deck preparatory to leaving the stricken vessel.

Captain Dreyer giving final orders from the bridge shortly before the ship turned turtle.

These exclusive " Daily Mirror " photographs illustrate vividly a sea drama which added to the long record of the heroism of ship captains. The Monte Cervantes, a liner only three years old, with her hull insured for £200,000, went ashore near Tierra del Fuego, in the Straits of Magellan, South America, and became almost completely submerged on the following day. After seeing to the safety of his 1,500 passengers and crew, Captain Dreyer refused to be rescued and went down with the ship he commanded. The survivors were seven hours in open boats before they reached the shore of the isl Ushaia, an Argentine prison colony. See also pages 12 and 13.

JOIN THE PROSPERITY PARTY TO-DAY:
ENROLMENT FORM ON P. 4

GRAMOPHONE NOTES TO-DAY

Daily Mirror
THE DAILY PICTURE PAPER WITH THE LARGEST NET SALE

No. 8,193   Registered at the G.P.O. as a Newspaper.   THURSDAY, FEBRUARY 20, 1930   One Penny

£500 PICTURE PUZZLE WEEKLY

SUPERSTITION OF A BRIDE

A WIFE SOLD FOR £17

Mme. Marcel Leppic giving evidence in a Paris court, where her husband, a Russian workman, was sentenced to a month's imprisonment and fined 8s. on a charge of selling her for £17 to his rival, an Estonian named Alex Michk (seated), who was fined 16s. for entering into an illegal transaction.—("Daily Mirror" photographs.)

Miss Loelia Ponsonby making a detour to avoid passing under a ladder when on her final shopping expedition in Bond-street yesterday before her marriage to the Duke of Westminster (right), which will take place in London to-day.

Marcel Leppic. He wanted to pay his fare to America.

WOMAN'S HUGE TASK

Dr. Lambert, chosen as Chairman of the newly-constituted Central Public Health Committee of the L.C.C. Her job involves great responsibilities, including control of 75,000 hospital beds.

WINTER SPORTS PARTY HELD UP IN MOUNTAIN VILLAGE

Cars and coaches which took a great number of winter sports visitors, including a large party of English people, from Nice to Piera Cava, a mountain village, where they were cut off from the outer world by a snowfall and a landslide for thirty hours. They were given shelter for the night in barracks.

THE DAILY MIRROR, Friday, February 21, 1930.

GREAT RUSH TO ENROL IN NEW PARTY

Daily Mirror

THE DAILY PICTURE PAPER WITH THE LARGEST NET SALE

No. 8,194   Registered at the G.P.O. as a Newspaper.   FRIDAY, FEBRUARY 21, 1930   One Penny

DUKE'S TEN-MINUTE MARRIAGE CEREMONY

Bride and bridegroom after their marriage. The room where the ceremony was held contained furniture from the Duke's town house.

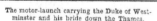

The motor-launch carrying the Duke of Westminster and his bride down the Thames.

At Westminster Pier on the way to the motor-launch, which the Duke piloted.

The Duke and his bride going aboard the yacht, in which the wedding breakfast was held.—("Daily Mirror" photographs.)

In a ceremony lasting ten minutes the Duke of Westminster was married yesterday at the City of Westminster Union Office to Miss Loelia Ponsonby, daughter of Sir Frederick Ponsonby, the King's Treasurer. After a brief visit to a reception at the bride's home at St. James's Palace, the Duke and Duchess boarded a motor-launch at Westminster and, escorted by two speed boats, travelled to Deptford to the luxurious yacht the Cutty Sark, in which they left on their way to the Riviera. See also page 28.

23

GREAT MYSTERY SERIAL BEGINS ON MONDAY

DailyMirror

THE DAILY PICTURE PAPER WITH THE LARGEST NET SALE

No. 8,195   Registered at the G.P.O. as a Newspaper.   **SATURDAY, FEBRUARY 22, 1930**   One Penny

KAYE DON'S 4,000-h.p. CAR FOR RECORD QUEST

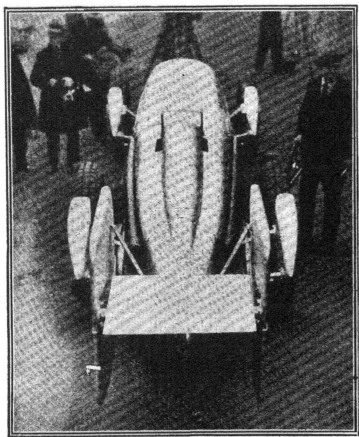

A back view of the car, showing the two longitudinal stabilising fins.

A pivoting 'plane to be used as an air brake.

Mr. Kaye Don at the wheel, which is removed to let him get in.

"Daily Mirror" photographs of Mr. Kaye Don's amazing British car, Silver Bullet, which he will take on board the Berengaria when he sails for America on Wednesday in quest of the world's land speed record, held by Sir Henry Segrave. He is confident it has sufficient power to reach 240 to 250 m.p.h. It measures 31ft. in length, and some remarkable features are an ice-box engine-cooling system, fireproof bulkhead and a steel frame over 13in. deep at one point.

MANY INSURANCE CLAIMS PAID: REGISTER NOW

Daily Mirror

THE DAILY PICTURE PAPER WITH THE LARGEST NET SALE

No. 8,197   Registered at the G.P.O. as a Newspaper.   TUESDAY, FEBRUARY 25, 1930   One Penny

ACTRESS TO MARRY A RACING MOTORIST

Miss Jane Baxter, whose engagement to Mr. Clive Dunfee, the racing motorist, is announced, photographed with her fiancé at the Shaftesbury Theatre, where she is playing in "The Middle Watch."

STUDENT EXILE RETURNS

Antonio Sbert addressing the demonstrators.

COUNCIL ACT TOWN'S HISTORY

The Mayor of Abingdon, Berks, Councillor F. Gibson (X), in "Scenes from Abingdon History," which is being produced there this week. The corporation are also appearing. The administering of justice in 1689 is represented above.

PEER'S STATEMENT

Lord Brownlow, president of Grantham Conservative and Unionist Association, has revealed that at a meeting of 500 Conservatives at the Junior Carlton Club the majority were in favour of Empire Free Trade.

HELD A SUSPECT

Mrs. Dora Causton, the widowed mother of two children, held a man who was alleged to have climbed from her St. Pancras flat through a window on to the balcony. A man friend seized another man. The police detained two men.

Part of the enormous and enthusiastic crowd of students who welcomed their leader, Antonio Sbert, back in Madrid. He had been exiled during General Primo de Rivera's dictatorship. Youths from Madrid and the provinces escorted him to the university buildings.

£1,000 ZIG-ZAG PUZZLE: PRIZEWINNERS' NAMES

Daily Mirror

THE DAILY PICTURE PAPER WITH THE LARGEST NET SALE

No. 8,199   Registered at the G.P.O. as a Newspaper.   THURSDAY, FEBRUARY 27, 1930   One Penny

EAST END CHILDREN WELCOME THE QUEEN

Union Jacks waved merrily by a guard of honour of small children as a greeting to the Queen on her arrival at the West Ham Central Mission, Barking-road, E., yesterday.

The occasion was the twenty-fifth anniversary of the women's meetings. Large crowds cheered the royal car in the streets.—("Daily Mirror" photograph.)

SIR A. FRIPP DEAD

Sir Alfred Fripp, the surgeon, who died yesterday at Lulworth Cove, Dorset, aged sixty-four. He was known as "Frothblower No. 1." He had been honorary surgeon-in-ordinary to the King since 1910.—("Daily Mirror.")

The Queen and billiards players with whom she conversed at the Men's Club. She also visited the Girls' Club, Angas Institute, Rest-a-While (home for old people) and Marnham House Settlement.

"FROM I O U TO £ s. d.": BY VISCOUNT ROTHERMERE

FREE HAMPERS WINNERS' NAMES

DailyMirror

THE DAILY PICTURE PAPER WITH THE LARGEST NET SALE

SPECIAL EDITION

No. 8,201   Registered at the G.P.O. as a Newspaper.   SATURDAY, MARCH 1, 1930   One Penny

SCOTT-SHARKEY FIGHT—PICTURE BY CABLE

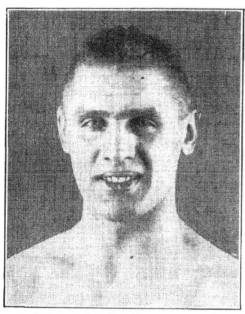

Phil Scott who lost his fight at Miami Florida, with—

—Jack Sharkey, the referee awarding a technical knock-out.

Phil Scott on his left knee as the referee stands over him counting. This picture, the first of the fight to reach England, was received by the Bartlane process (Western Union transmission). The "Daily Mirror" sent Bartlane machines and a staff of operators to Miami.

Gene Tunney, former holder of the championship, said: "I think Scott quit."

Jimmy Johnston, Scott's American manager, who had protested against the referee's powers.

Lou Magnolia, referee, against whose decision on a technicality protests are being made.

Max Schmeling, German champion, will be Sharkey's next opponent—in New York.

The pros and cons of the referee's decision in the Scott-Sharkey heavyweight championship fight at Miami, Florida, were hotly debated yesterday throughout the world. Witnesses gave conflicting opinions of incidents which led up to Scott being declared the loser, without being counted out, in the third round. The fight was something of a financial fiasco, the gate being at least £10,000 less than was expected. As a result the boxers' purses will be greatly reduced.

27

PASSENGER TRAIN IN FATAL SMASH IN TUNNEL

RADIO NOTES TO-DAY

DailyMirror

THE DAILY PICTURE PAPER WITH THE LARGEST NET SALE

No. 8,206 — Registered at the G.P.O. as a Newspaper. — FRIDAY, MARCH 7, 1930 — One Penny

£1,000 RACING COUPON

HEROIC RESCUES IN FRENCH FLOOD HORROR

Waist deep in water—rescuing a woman and a civilian.

Collapsed houses at Montauban after the swollen waters of the Tarn subsided.

M. Louis Bosquet, who rescued 150 people at Montauban.

Soldiers carrying women to safety on their shoulders.

A railway embankment breached. The rails are hanging over a void.

The terrible floods that have laid waste rich wine districts in the South-West of France have been marked by many instances of heroism, some rescuers, however, paying for their bravery with their lives. It is feared that the death roll is at least 800, and 10,000 people are homeless. Many villages are practically wiped out near Montauban, a quarter of which has been destroyed. President Doumergue and M. Tardieu, the Premier, will go to the stricken region to-day.—("Daily Mirror" photographs.)

SPRING FASHIONS NUMBER ON MONDAY: 32 PAGES

DailyMirror

THE DAILY PICTURE PAPER WITH THE LARGEST NET SALE

No. 8,207 — Registered at the G.P.O. as a Newspaper. — SATURDAY, MARCH 8, 1930 — One Penny

PEER'S MANSION ON FIRE—LABORATORY LOSS

Lady Rayleigh superintending the return of goods which were taken from Terling Place, the seat of Lord Rayleigh, near Witham, Essex, during fire yesterday.

STATE POST FOR GIRL OF 20

Mlle. Odette Peret, aged twenty, and her father, M. Raoul Peret, French Minister of Justice, to whom she is private secretary. It is the first time a girl so young has filled such a post in France.

Damage done by the fire. The left wing of the premises was destroyed, but the mansion itself was unaffected.

Lord Rayleigh and his daughter, the Hon. Daphne Strutt, collecting valuable books.

Lord Rayleigh's laboratory, in which were many instruments, was burned out during the fire at Terling Place yesterday, but a number of books containing valuable data were saved. Servants and villagers removed much of the furniture from the building.—("Daily Mirror" photographs.)

ALL WEEK-END SPORT IN NEWS AND PICTURES

SPRING FASHIONS NUMBER

DailyMirror

THE DAILY PICTURE PAPER WITH THE LARGEST NET SALE

32 PAGES

No. 8,208   Registered at the G.P.O. as a Newspaper.   MONDAY, MARCH 10, 1930   One Penny

THAMES TRAGEDY INQUIRY? | A SPRING NOTE

Wreckage off Southend of the Dutch schooner Oranje, which sank a month ago with the loss of two lives. Inset, Pieter van der Leigh (clean-shaven), the only survivor, and Mr. E. Cotgrove, berthing master at Southend, who observed the schooner's plight, and says he appealed to coastguards to call out the lifeboat. It is strongly rumoured that an inquiry will be held. (See news story.)

ONE DEAD, FOUR HURT IN HYDE PARK CAR SMASH

Miss Brenda Lazarus, multiple cuts.

Mr. Eric Lazarus has since died.

The wrecked saloon car. Inset, Mr. P. Lazarus, stockbroker, of Elvaston-place.

After colliding with another car, a big saloon motor-car dashed into a tree in Hyde Park, and turned turtle. Three of the four occupants—Mr. Philip Lazarus, his son and daughter, and the chauffeur—were pinned underneath the car and firemen used axes to release them. A man in the other vehicle was also hurt.

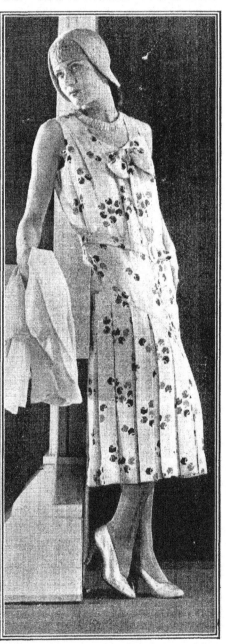

A sleeveless semi-sports model by Baroque of ivory crepe de Chine with design in brown, orange and green — one of many smart models with which this Spring Fashions number is illustrated. See also pages 14, 16 and 17.—("Daily Mirror" photograph.)

MORE GUINEAS FOR MOTORISTS ON SUNDAY NEXT

GRAMOPHONE
NOTES
TO-DAY

Daily Mirror
THE DAILY PICTURE PAPER WITH THE LARGEST NET SALE

No. 8,211   Registered at the G.P.O. as a Newspaper.   THURSDAY, MARCH 13, 1930   One Penny

WIRELESS
PROGRAMMES
ON PAGE 19

ROOM 66 MYSTERY

Mrs. Rosaline Fox, for the alleged murder of whom her son, Sidney Harry Fox (inset) is on trial at Lewes. She was found dead in a smoke-filled room, Room 66, at a Margate hotel. Fox yesterday pleaded not guilty.

EMPIRE TRADE PLEAS

Sir Herbert Austin.

Sir Robert Horne, M.P.   Sir Wm. Alexander.   Mr. L. S. Amery, M.P.

At a National Union of Manufacturers meeting at Central Hall, Westminster, to-day Mr. Amery will move a resolution urging the extension of Empire trade by preferential duties and the necessity for duties on manufactured foreign goods. Sir R. Horne will move a resolution favouring McKenna duties. Brigadier-General Sir W. Alexander and Sir H. Austin will be seconders.

4,000-YEAR-OLD COFFIN FOUND—SKELETON WHICH MAY BE THAT OF A PRINCESS

The superintendent measuring the skeleton in the mortuary.

The coffin, which measures 7ft. by 3ft.

A sandstone coffin found during excavations near the old church at Beddington, Surrey, is possibly a relic of 4,000 years ago. Inside were the almost complete skeleton of a young woman, who may have been a British princess, and remains of two bone candle- sticks. The skeleton may be of medical interest; only one of the teeth, which are well preserved, is missing. Search is being made for any other ancient relics there may be in the neighbourhood.—("Daily Mirror" photographs.)

MORE GUINEAS FOR MOTORISTS ON SUNDAY

150 FREE HAMPERS WINNERS' NAMES

Daily Mirror

THE DAILY PICTURE PAPER WITH THE LARGEST NET SALE

No. 8,213   Registered at the G.P.O. as a Newspaper.   SATURDAY, MARCH 15, 1930   One Penny

WIRELESS PROGRAMMES ON PAGE 17

CALCUTTA CUP SURPRISE

J. G. Askew, who was announced to be unfit last night.

J. C. Hubbard, the Harlequins player, who will take Askew's place.

P. W. Brook, selected yesterday to fill the vacancy left in the pack.

B. H. Black, badly hurt in inter-collegiate final, Oxford, is now fit.

The news that Askew would not play for England in the match against Scotland—the Rugby season climax—at Twickenham to-day was a big surprise. It will be Hubbard's first international.

WEIRD STATUE

CHANNEL TUNNEL IN SIGHT AT LAST—SCHEME APPROVED

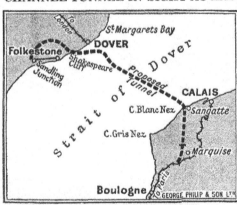

How the proposed tunnel would join England and France.

The late Mr. William Low, of Wrexham, who was the originator of the Channel Tunnel scheme and prepared the first plans in 1866.

The top of an almost completely filled-in shaft at the foot of the Shakespeare Cliff, Dover. It is all that remains of work done in connection with Channel Tunnel plans in 1885. The Committee of Inquiry set up by the Government expresses complete approval of the scheme in a report issued yesterday.

A strange statue recently set up on a high brick pedestal in a new quarter of Breslau in Germany. It represents the Holy Virgin carrying her Child and astride a donkey, as during the flight into Egypt. The smaller picture shows the human figures.

THE DAILY MIRROR, Friday, March 21, 1930.

RACING NUMBER ON MONDAY: SPECIAL FEATURES

BEST FAMILY INSURANCE

DailyMirror

THE DAILY PICTURE PAPER WITH THE LARGEST NET SALE

32 PAGES

No. 8,218   Registered at the G.P.O. as a Newspaper.   FRIDAY, MARCH 21, 1930   One Penny

MAN AND WIFE ON A FLIGHT TO CAPETOWN

Friends waving good-bye as a twin-engine biplane, in which Mr. and Mrs. A. S. Butler are attempting a flight to Capetown, left Heston Aerodrome yesterday. Mrs. Butler is acting as reserve pilot.

FOX TRIAL EVIDENCE CLASH

Sir B. Spilsbury.   Dr. Bronte.

Professor Sydney Smith.

At yesterday's hearing of the murder charge against Sidney Harry Fox at Lewes Professor Sydney Smith, of Edinburgh University, rejected Sir Bernard Spilsbury's view that Mrs. Fox was strangled. Dr. Bronté, the pathologist, said that in his opinion Mrs. Fox died of heart failure caused by disease accelerated by shock.

Mr. Butler handing his wife a lifebelt as she entered the aeroplane in readiness to depart.

BRIDAL WRAP AGAINST COLD

The bride wearing a wrap when leaving with the bridegroom after the wedding of Mr. Geoffrey Snagge and Miss Norah Longfield at St. Peter's, Eaton-square, yesterday.

33

FIRST PICTURES OF GANDHI'S MARCH ON PAGE 24

WIRELESS PROGRAMMES ON PAGE 19

Daily Mirror

THE DAILY PICTURE PAPER WITH THE LARGEST NET SALE

No. 8,223   Registered at the G.P.O. as a Newspaper.   THURSDAY, MARCH 27, 1930   One Penny

£500 FOR 18 RESULTS SEE PAGE 23

OUTSIDER WINS THE LINCOLN FOR FRANCE

M. Boussac, the owner of Leonidas II.

H. Southey, who rode Leonidas II to victory.

The French horse Slipper, favourite, in the parade.

Leonidas II after its surprise victory. It was perfectly fresh in the unsaddling enclosure.

The finish of the Lincolnshire Handicap yesterday, the 66 to 1 outsider Leonidas II passing the winning post three lengths ahead of Culzean, with Knight Error two lengths further away. And so, although the French favourite Slipper badly failed, France scored a victory in the race for the third time in seven years. The winner came across the Channel last year for the Kempton Park Jubilee, but was scratched at the eleventh hour.—("Daily Mirror" photographs.)

THE DAILY MIRROR, Saturday, March 29, 1930

BEST FAMILY INSURANCE: REGISTER TO-DAY

DailyMirror

THE DAILY PICTURE PAPER WITH THE LARGEST NET SALE

No. 8,225   Registered at the G.P.O. as a Newspaper.   SATURDAY, MARCH 29, 1930   One Penny

IRISH TRIUMPH IN A GREAT GRAND NATIONAL

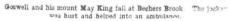

Goswell and his mount May King fall at Beechers Brook. The jockey was hurt and helped into an ambulance.

Shaun Goilin, owned by Mr. W. Midwood (inset), winning the Grand National by a neck.

The first fence. The winning owner achieved his ambition with a horse that once changed hands for £23—after failing with Silvo, which cost him 10,500 guineas.

One of the most exciting Grand Nationals ever seen led yesterday to one of the closest finishes on record. Out of a field of forty-one only five horses finished. Grakle, the favourite, fell. On the flat it was a magnificent struggle between the first three horses.

Shaun Goilin's win was an Irish triumph, for not only is the jockey an Irishman, but the trainer, Frank Hartigan, is a Tipperary man. The horse, says the owner, is thoroughly Irish. See also pages 12 and 13.

35

FAMOUS GENERAL AND THE DEATH PENALTY

DailyMirror

THE DAILY PICTURE PAPER WITH THE LARGEST NET SALE

No. 8,226   Registered at the G.P.O. as a Newspaper.   MONDAY, MARCH 31, 1930   One Penny

SUBMARINE GOES ASHORE ON CORNISH COAST

The submarine L 1 ashore at St. Just, Cornwall. She lies on an even keel and is very little damaged. She was built during the war and had been sold out of the service. It is supposed that she was in tow at the time she ran ashore.

VICAR AT WORK IN HIS DOLLS' HOSPITAL

The Rev. F. E. Coope, of Haywards Heath, Sussex, in his dolls' hospital. He is an expert dolls' doctor and has advertised in the parish magazine asking for long golden hair with which to repair bald heads. The present hair fashion has affected his supply. Children may bring dolls to him on Sunday mornings for operations and rejuvenation.—("Daily Mirror" photographs.)

SHOOTING VIEWS

Brigadier-General F. P. Crozier, who writes to the "Daily Mirror" protesting against the death penalty for cowardice on active service being abolished in the Army and R.A.F. The suggestion, he says, is a thoroughly mischievous bit of claptrap.

BATHING COSTUME FEATURE TO-DAY: PAGES 2, 16, 17

£870 IN PRIZES WON BY READERS

Daily Mirror

THE DAILY PICTURE PAPER WITH THE LARGEST NET SALE

No. 8,232   Registered at the G.P.O. as a Newspaper.   MONDAY, APRIL 7, 1930   One Penny

32 PAGES

GANDHI'S DEFIANCE

Reginald Reynolds, a British follower of Gandhi.

Mahatma Gandhi, the Indian Nationalist leader.

What Gandhi expected to be the first law-breaking move of his anti-British campaign in India has been made. He and his followers filled pots with sea water and obtained salt residue. The authorities take the view that as the salt was unfit for human consumption no infringement of Salt Laws took place.

VETERAN M.P. TO MARRY FOURTH WIFE

Mr. Will Thorne, the veteran Socialist M.P. for West Ham, and Miss Beatrice Collins, to whom he is engaged to be married. Miss Collins, who is forty-two, will be his fourth wife. He is seventy-two.

BLAZING ROOF THRILLS

A big crowd, many from Hyde Park, watch the outbreak.

Firemen with smoke masks about to enter a large building in Knightsbridge during a fierce fire which greatly damaged the roof yesterday.—("Daily Mirror" photographs.)

MANY INSURANCE CLAIMS PAID: REGISTER NOW

WIRELESS PROGRAMMES ON PAGE 19

Daily Mirror

THE DAILY PICTURE PAPER WITH THE LARGEST NET SALE

NEW SERIAL TO-MORROW

No. 8,233   Registered at the G.P.O. as a Newspaper.   TUESDAY, APRIL 8, 1930   One Penny

HERO'S REWARD

ROYAL DUKE'S GOLDEN KEY

Admiral Sir Roger Keyes presenting the silver medal of the Royal National Lifeboat Institution to Coxswain H. Griggs, junr., of Hythe, Kent, at a general meeting of the governors at Caxton Hall, yesterday.—("Daily Mirror.")

CHILDREN'S MEET TO END THE SEASON

Colonel Greene, the Master, giving hints at the children's meet, which yesterday wound up the Cottesmore Hunt's season, at Edmondthorpe Hall, Leicestershire.

The Duke of Gloucester opening the door of the new buildings of the Surrey County Hall at Kingston yesterday. He used a golden key in the presence of 800 guests. The buildings are of steel and concrete, with stone facings.

BEGIN OUR NEW SERIAL STORY TO-DAY: PAGE 17

WIRELESS PROGRAMMES ON PAGE 23

DailyMirror

THE DAILY PICTURE PAPER WITH THE LARGEST NET SALE

£10,000 FREE INSURANCE

No. 8,235   Registered at the G.P.O. as a Newspaper.   THURSDAY, APRIL 10, 1930   One Penny

BOY AND GIRL DRAMA

GOLF COURSE "BEARD"

Lilian Smith.

George Collier.

At Mortlake Police Court yesterday George Collier, aged fifteen, was committed for trial on a charge of attempting to murder Lilian Smith by strangling her on Sheen Common. "I only wished to frighten her," he said. Bail was refused.

PEER AND THREATS AGAINST HIS LIFE

Lord Brentford (hands on table) with Lord Danesfort, President of the British Empire Union, before a meeting of the union in London last night. Earlier in the day a threatening telephone message was received by Lord Brentford, and a policeman was on duty outside the meeting.

A divot thrown up by Archie Compston at Roehampton Club yesterday rises into a position which gives him the appearance of having a beard.

G. Faulkner, who did record 65 at Roehampton. R. A. Whitcombe then did 64.

Lady Alness, wife of the Lord Justice Clerk of Scotland, taking part in a competition at Barnes yesterday. She was struck on the head by a golf ball and retired.

WEEK'S FREE HOLIDAY AT THE SEASIDE: SEE P. 4

Daily Mirror

THE DAILY PICTURE PAPER WITH THE LARGEST NET SALE

No. 8,238   Registered at the G.P.O. as a Newspaper.   MONDAY, APRIL 14, 1930   One Penny

YPRES CATHEDRAL OPENED—PICTURES BY AIR

A picture taken from a " Daily Mirror " aeroplane of the rebuilt Cathedral at Ypres, after it had been opened yesterday and the ruins of the Cloth Hall

The ruins of the Cathedral during the last year of the war.

Abbé J. Vermaut (X), dean of the Cathedral, in the procession from Elverdinghe.

Two of the pictures above and another on page 28 were brought to London yesterday by " Daily Mirror " aeroplane. The opening of Ypres Cathedral for services was preceded by a procession with palms from the temporary church at Elverdinghe, and Abbé J. Ver- maut celebrated the first Mass. Hundreds of English people attended the ceremony. It has taken over seven years to rebuild the Cathedral, which is on the site of the one de- stroyed in the war and is modelled on the same plans.

BOUVERIE GIVES 14 WINNERS IN TWO DAYS

WIRELESS PROGRAMMES ON PAGE 23

DailyMirror

THE DAILY PICTURE PAPER WITH THE LARGEST NET SALE

No. 8,240   Registered at the G.P.O. as a Newspaper.   WEDNESDAY, APRIL 16, 1930   One Penny

SHOW CATTLE LOST IN FIRE

A twenty-man engine being used to fight a fire at Streetly Hall, near West Wickham, Cambridgeshire, yesterday. Twelve head of cattle and several pigs, all of pedigree strain, intended for show purposes, were lost, and some farm machinery and buildings were destroyed. The farm manager jumped into a pond to extinguish his burning clothes.

LINER STOPS TO SAVE DROWNING DOG

Captain A. D. Turton, who, turning the Clan liner, Clan Macnab, round in the Bay of Biscay, steamed back and rescued a foxhound which had fallen overboard apparently half an hour before the incident was reported to him.—("Daily Mirror.")

STOLEN MEDALS RETURNED

Mr. Edward Smallwood with his dead sons' medals which were stolen from his house at Highbury and were sent to a weekly paper with a note asking for them to be re-turned to the owner.

PODMORE SEES HIS WIFE

Mrs. W. H. Podmore (side-faced) reading a telegram sent from Winchester Gaol to Mr. C. Dukes, M.P. (centre), giving her permission yesterday to visit her husband, who is under sentence of death for the South-ampton murder. She spent an hour with her husband.

TAX PROTEST

Sir Perceval Laurence, a former Puisne Judge of the Supreme Court of South Africa, protested in his £273,521 will that death duties are "fero-cious fines."

OBITUARY

Sir Edward Pollock, who died yesterday at his London residence, at the age of eighty-eight, was for thirty-seven years an official referee of the Supreme Court.

41

THE DAILY MIRROR Saturday, April 19, 1930.

BEST HOLIDAY INSURANCE: REGISTER TO-DAY

DailyMirror

THE DAILY PICTURE PAPER WITH THE LARGEST NET SALE

No. 8,242   Registered at the C.P.O. as a Newspaper.   SATURDAY, APRIL 19, 1930   One Penny

THE START OF AN "OVERCOAT" HOLIDAY

Holidaymakers clad in warm coats on the chilly front at Brighton yesterday.

Ramblers taking refreshment before their departure from Derby for a holiday jaunt in the Peak District yesterday.—("Daily Mirror.")

BRAVE GIRL UNDER AN OMNIBUS

Miss Elsie Smith, aged eighteen, of Greenhithe, in Charing Cross Hospital yesterday suffering from a broken leg and head injuries sustained when she became pinned for fifteen minutes under an omnibus in St. Martin's-place. She smiled and talked while she was being released by firemen.

The entertainment of the band on the beach at Eastbourne.

Expecting fine and warm weather from a late Easter greater numbers of people than usual are spending the first break of the year at the seaside. In some places, however, yesterday was the coldest Good Friday for years. Rather cold weather is forecast. See pages 10 and 11.

HAVE YOU SENT YOUR "FREE HOLIDAY POSTCARD?"

WIRELESS PROGRAMMES ON PAGE 18

Daily Mirror

THE DAILY PICTURE PAPER WITH THE LARGEST NET SALE

NEW £500 CONTEST TO-DAY

No. 8,243   Registered at the G.P.O. as a Newspaper.   MONDAY, APRIL 21, 1930   One Penny

SUN SHINES IN SOUTH BUT SHUNS LONDON

A military band playing to empty seats in the Park. The "silence" notice adds an amusing touch to the scene.

Sharing a rug in Hyde Park.

The bride wears a sou'-wester after the wedding of Mr. C. Fin and Miss E. Frankland at St. Albans.

A mounted policeman on duty has Rotten Row all to himself.

Basking in sunshine, quite bright if not really warm, at Hastings.

South Coast resorts enjoyed sunshine yesterday, although the people who in almost unprecedented numbers flocked to the seaside for Easter have not yet received the full reward their optimism certainly deserves. In London rain again held unwelcome sway, and it was an indoor holiday in the capital. And yet, just off the West Coast, summerlike conditions reign over the Atlantic Ocean! Experts hold out little hope of the fine weather area reaching this country to-day. See also pages 12 and 13.

43

£500 RACING CONTEST: FINAL COUPON TO-DAY

DailyMirror

THE DAILY PICTURE PAPER WITH THE LARGEST NET SALE

No. 8,244 — Registered at the G.P.O as a Newspaper — TUESDAY, APRIL 22, 1930 — One Penny

FIVE KILLED IN CALCUTTA RIOTS | DROWNED

Police moving dismantled buffalo carts to allow the passage of traffic after the serious conflicts which arose in Calcutta following passive resistance demonstrations by buffalo cart drivers. Five Indians were killed and 100 people were injured. The carters objected to being restrained from taking out their buffaloes during the hottest hours.

Mr. Crosbie Garstin, of Penzance, the well-known author, drowned in Salcombe Harbour when a boat in which he was making for a yacht capsized. A woman friend and a deck hand with him at the time were saved. He had been rancher, miner, ranger and soldier.

TO DESCRIBE THE TESTS

Mr. C. G. Macartney, the famous Australian cricketer, coming to England at the special request of the "Daily Mirror" to describe the Tests, arrives at Southampton to-day. His articles will appear in no other English morning news

LAP RECORD BEATEN AT BROOKLANDS BY CAPTAIN BIRKIN

The Hon. Dorothy Paget's 4½-litre supercharged Bentley, driven by Captain H. R. S. Birkin (inset), at Brooklands yesterday. With a speed of 135.33 m.p.h. he beat the lap record of 134.23 m.p.h., held by Mr. Kaye Don, who will arrive back from America to-morrow. Captain Birkin also won the Bedford Handicap (6½ miles), from scratch, at 117.81 m.p.h.

44

THE DAILY MIRROR, Saturday, April 26, 1930

TO-DAY'S CUP FINAL IN NEWS AND PICTURES

DailyMirror

THE DAILY PICTURE PAPER WITH THE LARGEST NET SALE

No. 8,248   Registered at the G.P.O. as a Newspaper.   SATURDAY, APRIL 26, 1930   One Penny

THE PRINCE HOME AFTER 18,000-MILE TOUR

The Prince of Wales leaving the liner at Marseilles to start his flight to England yesterday.

Getting into the aeroplane, which Squadron-Leader Don piloted.

With Lord Tyrrell, the British Ambassador, at the officers' mess at Le Bourget, Paris.

The Prince's aeroplane making a perfect landing at his private landing place near Fort Belvedere, his new home at Sunningdale, on the completion of his journey from Marseilles, which occupied eight hours and a half, and included stops at Lyons and Le Bourget. While a R.A.F. escort circled in salute the Prince was greeted by the Duke of York, Prince George and a group of friends. Inset, the Prince going to the King's car, which took him to Fort Belvedere, where the King and Queen were waiting. Her Majesty eagerly walked half across a field to welcome her son. Thus with quiet informality ended the Prince's 18,000 miles journey and expedition in African wilds.

45

WOMAN READER WINS £500 PUZZLE PRIZE

WIRELESS PROGRAMMES ON PAGE 18

DailyMirror

THE DAILY PICTURE PAPER WITH THE LARGEST NET SALE

No. 8,249 — Registered at the G.P.O. as a Newspaper. — MONDAY, APRIL 28, 1930 — One Penny

£1,000 RACING CONTEST

OLD COMRADES' CAVALRY MEMORIAL TRIBUTE

The crowd round the Cavalry Memorial in Hyde Park where a wreath was deposited by Field-Marshal Viscount Allenby for the Combined Cavalry "Old Comrades."

GIRL OF NINETEEN COMMANDS A BARGE

Lord Allenby (B) beside the wreath with Lord Baden-Powell (A). A procession, headed by the Band of the Life Guards, passed across the Park. Former cavalrymen from many parts of the country attended the ceremony.—("Daily Mirror" photographs.)

Miss Lizzie Meadows, aged nineteen, the skipper, on her barge Lioness, now at Paddington Basin, with her sister, aged seven, and her brother, aged twelve. She has successfully divided her time between commanding the barge and mothering her young relations since her parents died three years ago. All this in spite of her loss of one leg.—("Daily Mirror" photograph.)

C. G. MACARTNEY DESCRIBES AUSTRALIA'S FIRST MATCH

WIRELESS PROGRAMMES ON PAGE 19

DailyMirror

THE DAILY PICTURE PAPER WITH THE LARGEST NET SALE

No. 8,252   Registered at the G.P.O. as a Newspaper.   THURSDAY, MAY 1, 1930   One Penny

£500 PICTURE PUZZLE WEEKLY

THE AUSTRALIANS' FIRST MATCH IN ENGLAND

Above, A. Jackson (Australia) caught by C. F. Walters off Brooke after scoring 24; below, D. Bradman batting.

D. J. Bradman scored 75 not out. His batting was forceful.

W. M. Woodfull, the Australian captain, driving to the boundary. He scored 95 not out.

A. Fairfax, who took four Worcestershire wickets for 36 runs.

M. F. S. Jewell, the captain of Worcestershire, caught by A. Fairfax, off C. V. Grimmett, after having scored 7 runs.

The Australians made a very satisfactory showing in their first match in England, which started yesterday against Worcestershire at Worcester. The home team batted first and were all out for 131. W. M. Woodfull handled the Australian side well and the fielding was bright. The visitors scored 199 for the loss of one wicket. The Worcestershire bowling was poor. The weather was very fine and the wicket was of the slow, easy type. C. G. Macartney's description of the match is on page 2.

THE DAILY MIRROR, Tuesday, May 6, 1930.

MANY INSURANCE CLAIMS PAID: REGISTER NOW

WIRELESS PROGRAMMES ON PAGE 19

DailyMirror

THE DAILY PICTURE PAPER WITH THE LARGEST NET SALE

SPECIAL EDITION

No. 8,256   Registered at the G.P.O. as a Newspaper.   TUESDAY, MAY 6, 1930   One Penny

FIVE DEAD AND 100 HURT IN EXPLOSION

A rescued workman, his head in bandages, describing his experiences.

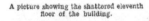

A picture showing the shattered eleventh floor of the building.

EX-P.M.G. SECEDES

Lord Illingworth, former P.M.G. in Mr. Lloyd George's war administration, who has joined the Conservatives. He states he is unable to support the present Liberal policy.

Firemen and others on the eleventh floor of Bibby's Oil Cake Mills, Liverpool, where five people were killed and about 100 injured in an explosion which occurred yesterday. The upper part of the building was enveloped in flames. In another part of Liverpool yesterday thirteen people were gassed when cylinders burst in a stable yard in Slade-street.—(Pictures by "Daily Mirror" photo-telephony.)

POLICE STONED BY MOB IN BOMBAY: PAGE 3

WIRELESS PROGRAMMES ON PAGE 17

Daily Mirror

THE DAILY PICTURE   NEWSPAPER WITH THE LARGEST NET SALE

No. 8,258   Registered at the G.P.O. as a Newspaper.   THURSDAY, MAY 8, 1930   One Penny

£500 PICTURE PUZZLE WEEKLY

POLICE ROOF-BESIEGER KICKED SENSELESS

Albert Ladlow shaking a fire escape in an effort to prevent a policeman from reaching him.

Sergeant Evans, in plain clothes, reaches the top of the fire escape.

Bringing down Sergeant Evans, unconscious after being kicked on the head.

A policeman trying to step over Sergeant Evans, senseless on the escape.

In full view of thousands of people, a dozen policemen yesterday besieged a young man, Albert Ladlow, who had taken refuge on a roof in Gales-gardens, Bethnal Green. Firemen were also called. Ladlow, who had been under medical attention, climbed to his refuge when the relieving officer called. Finally, seeing that escape was impossible, he slid from the roof, fell 30ft., and was picked up unconscious and taken to hospital.— ("Daily Mirror" photographs.)

THE DAILY MIRROR, Friday, May 9, 1930.

BIG CASUALTY ROLL IN RIOTS IN INDIAN TOWN

Daily Mirror

THE DAILY PICTURE PAPER WITH THE LARGEST NET SALE

No. 8,259   Registered at the G.P.O. as a Newspaper.   FRIDAY, MAY 9, 1930   One Penny

THE QUEEN'S HAPPY HOUR AMONG CHILDREN

The Queen delighted by small pupils at play at the children's school, after she had opened yesterday the Rachel McMillan College for the training of girls in nursery work, Deptford.

6 WICKETS FOR 5

P. M. Hornibrook, the Australian left-handed bowler, who took six Essex wickets for five runs yesterday. His record for the innings was six wickets for eleven.—("Daily Mirror.")

Passing in front of mothers and babies. Next her is Miss M. McMillan, sister of the founder. The Queen has given active support to the scheme. She was greeted by 10,000 schoolchildren, who lined the streets. See also page 14.—("Daily Mirror" photographs.)

DIVORCE ECHO

Mr. A. C. Birch, of Lewisham, S.E., who had been divorced and under official pressure resigned his position as London County Council teacher. The case has caused much interest.

THE DAILY MIRROR, Saturday May 17, 1930.

BRITISH GOLF GIRL'S WIN AGAINST AMERICAN

£500
PICTURE
PUZZLE
WEEKLY

DailyMirror

THE DAILY PICTURE   PAPER WITH THE LARGEST NET SALE

No. 8,266   Registered at the G.P.O. as a Newspaper.   SATURDAY, MAY 17, 1930   One Penny

NEW
SERIAL
STARTS ON
MONDAY

BRITISH GIRL GOLFER BEATS U.S. CHAMPION

Miss Diana Fishwick, the new British open champion.

Miss Collett (also inset) putting at the eleventh green. She missed this and a great many other putts.

Miss Fishwick with the cup.—(By "Daily Mirror" photo-telephony.)

It was a triumph for Britain over America and for youth over experience when Miss Diana Fishwick, the nineteen-year-old North Foreland golfer, yesterday defeated Miss Glenna Collett, the U.S. champion, 4 and 3 in the final of the women's open championship. Her success is rendered the more notable by the fact that this was her first appearance in the championship. She was five up after eighteen holes. Miss Collett also reached the final last year, losing to Miss Joyce Wethered. See also page 20.

MANY INSURANCE CLAIMS PAID: REGISTER NOW

DailyMirror

THE DAILY PICTURE PAPER WITH THE LARGEST NET SALE

No. 8,268 | Registered at the G.P.O. as a Newspaper. | TUESDAY, MAY 20, 1930 | One Penny

SPECTACULAR FIRE AT THAMES-SIDE WHARF

Enormous clouds of choking smoke pouring yesterday evening from a flour warehouse that belongs to Messrs. H. R. Perry and Son, Commercial-road. Thousands of people—gathered on the opposite side of the Thames from Blackfriars to Waterloo Bridge—watched the outbreak. The smaller picture shows an injured fireman receiving a drink of water before being taken to hospital. See also page 24.

ROAD SAFETY BALLOT: £750 IN PRIZES

DAILY Mirror

THE DAILY PICTURE PAPER WITH THE LARGEST NET SALE

No. 8,271   Registered at the G.P.O. as a Newspaper.   FRIDAY, MAY 23, 1930   One Penny

THE KING AND QUEEN SEE VARIETY SHOW

Coram, the ventriloquist, and his dummy.

George Clarke in a baby car scored a big hit.—("Daily Mirror.")

THE LONE GIRL ACE'S PROGRESS

Miss Amy Johnson, who left Sourabaya, Java, yesterday, for Atamboea, about 750 miles away. Some uneasiness was felt when no news had been heard of her for over twelve hours.

The royal box decorated with garlands of roses.

The King and Queen with the Duke of Gloucester watching a Royal Command performance in aid of the Variety Artistes' Benevolent Fund at the Palladium last night. They laughed heartily at many of the jokes. Big crowds gathered outside the theatre for their arrival.

53

£750 ROAD SAFETY BALLOT: FULL DETAILS

WIRELESS PROGRAMMES ON PAGE 19

Daily Mirror

THE DAILY PICTURE PAPER WITH THE LARGEST NET SALE

No. 8,273   Registered at the G.P.O. as a Newspaper.   MONDAY, MAY 26, 1930   One Penny

NEW PICTURE PUZZLE TO-DAY

PROUD FAMILY OF THE EMPIRE'S HEROINE

Mrs. Johnson is the proudest woman in England now that her daughter Amy has reached Australia.

Triumphant Miss Amy Johnson, photographed in evening dress and again when turning her machine, has delighted her father (inset) and mother by her safe arrival in Australia. It was a happy coincidence that Miss Johnson's aeroplane landed at Port Darwin on Empire Day, after an epic flight from Croydon of nineteen days. The King immediately sent a telegram of congratulation. Although she failed to establish a record her feat in reaching Karachi in six days is unequalled. Her fortitude and skill are amazing when it is remembered that she covered hundreds of miles of wild country and sea. She is leaving Port Darwin with an air escort to-day for Sydney.

THE DAILY MIRROR, Wednesday, May 28, 1930.

YOUR CHANCE TO WIN £500 PRIZE: SEE PAGE 6

LAUGH DAILY WITH THE PATER

DailyMirror

THE DAILY PICTURE PAPER WITH THE LARGEST NET SALE

No. 8,275 — Registered at the G.P.O. as a Newspaper. — WEDNESDAY, MAY 28, 1930 — One Penny

£1,000 RACING COUPON TO-DAY

FLEET'S ADIEU TO CHIEF

FLOWERS FOR DUKE

Cheers from H.M.S. Warspite at Portsmouth for Admiral Sir Frederick Field, who yesterday relinquished his command of the Mediterranean Fleet to become First Sea Lord. Admiral Sir Ernie Chatfield succeeds him.

The Duke of York receiving flowers from Doreen Colman at the Manfield Orthopædic Hospital, Northampton, yesterday. He was entertained to a civic luncheon in connection with festival week.—("Daily Mirror.")

WALKING TOUR TRAGEDY

Mr. and Mrs. Leonard Gordon Murray before starting on a walking and cycling tour of Europe in 1926. Mr. Murray has arrived back in England after covering 10,000 miles, but Mrs. Murray died at Châlon-sur-Saône, France, and is buried there. —("Daily Mirror" photograph.)

BRITISH GIRL'S FORMIDABLE OPPONENT

Miss Mudford and, right, Mrs. Helen Wills Moody, to meet in the third round of women's singles in the French lawn tennis championships. Miss Mudford is an official member of a British team for the first time.

Admiral Sir F. Field acknowledging the cheers from Warspite.

THE DAILY MIRROR, Friday, May 30, 1930.

AMY JOHNSON'S ESCAPE WHEN 'PLANE CRASHES

WIRELESS PROGRAMMES ON PAGE 19

Daily Mirror

THE DAILY PICTURE — PAPER WITH THE LARGEST NET SALE

No. 8,277 — Registered at the G.P.O. as a Newspaper. — FRIDAY, MAY 30, 1930 — One Penny

£1,000 RACING CONTEST COUPON

THE QUEEN AND BABY PRINCESS AT OLYMPIA

Fencing display in the tournament.

The Queen and Princess Elizabeth watching the Royal Tournament at Olympia yesterday. During the musical drive of J Battery, R.H.A., the Princess danced up and down in time with the music, and when the gun teams drew up for the royal salute she stood and clapped vigorously. The royal party were most appreciative of the programme.—("Daily Mirror.")

The inspection of the guard of honour, carried out by the Duke of Gloucester and Prince George.

£750 BEST ROAD-USER BALLOT: RULES TO-DAY

DailyMirror

THE DAILY PICTURE — PAPER WITH THE LARGEST NET SALE

No. 8,279 — Registered at the G.P.O. as a Newspaper. — MONDAY, JUNE 2, 1930 — One Penny

SEVEN DEAD IN RAIL CRASH DUE TO SABOTAGE

The smash at Montereau, France, when a Paris-Nice express crashed into a workman's trolly deliberately placed across the metals. Seven people, among whom was a French woman from Hampstead, were killed, and eight, including three English women, were injured. Four of the front coaches left the rails.—("Daily Mirror.")

THE KING AND QUEEN AT ALBERT HALL CONCERT

The Royal Box at the Albert Hall yesterday when the King and Queen, with others of the Royal Family, attended the concert of the Philharmonic Symphony Orchestra of New York.

The trolly which was the cause of the accident.

MANY INSURANCE CLAIMS PAID: REGISTER NOW

FIRST DERBY NUMBER TO-MORROW

DailyMirror

THE DAILY PICTURE ● PAPER WITH THE LARGEST NET SALE

No. 8,280 — Registered at the G.P.O. as a Newspaper. — TUESDAY, JUNE 3, 1930 — One Penny

£100 CROSSWORD PUZZLE

AMY JOHNSON MADE C.B.E.—THREE NEW PEERS

Miss Amy Johnson, who is awarded the C.B.E. in the Birthday Honours announced this morning.

Mr. H. D. Gillies (with moustache), chief plastic surgeon to the Ministry of Pensions, is a new knight.

Mr. Henry Lytton, the famous member of the D'Oyly Carte Opera Company, becomes a Knight Bachelor.

Miss Margaret MacMillan, made Companion of Honour for services to Nursery School Movement.

Sir John Simon, Indian Statutory Commission chairman, becomes Knight Grand Commander of the Star of India.

Three peerages are created in the King's Birthday Honours, baronies being conferred upon Mr. Noel Buxton, M.P., Minister of Agriculture, Mr. H. S. Furniss, former Principal of Ruskin College, Oxford, and Sir Esmé Howard, former British Ambassador to U.S.A. There are three new baronets—Sir Leonard Dunning, Mr. Basil Mott and Mr. F. H. Royce. The Order of Merit is awarded to Dr. S. Alexander, the philosopher, Dr. M. R. James, the scholar, and Dr. G. M. Trevelyan, the historian.

THE DAILY MIRROR, Thursday, June 5, 1930.

CAMBRIDGE SHOOTING TRAGEDY REVELATIONS

£750 BALLOT COUPON TO-DAY

Daily Mirror

THE DAILY PICTURE   PAPER WITH THE LARGEST NET SALE

No. 8,282 — Registered at the G.P.O. as a Newspaper. — THURSDAY, JUNE 5, 1930 — One Penny

BEST DERBY PICTURES

THE AGA KHAN'S FIRST DERBY VICTORY

A "Daily Mirror" picture of the finish of the Derby at Epsom yesterday, when the Aga Khan's horse, Blenheim, who was an 18 to 1 chance and was ridden by H. Wragg, won by a length from Mr. S. Tattersall's Iliad. The favourite, Sir Hugo Hirst's Diolite, was third, and Major J. S. Courtauld's Silver Flare came in fourth. Seventeen ran.

The Aga Khan was also represented in the race by Rustom Pasha. It was his first Derby victory. The King and Queen saw the race, and others of the Royal Family also present were the Prince of Wales, the Duke of York, the Duke of Gloucester and Princess Mary Countess of Harewood. See also pages 12 and 13.

TEST ARTICLE BY MACARTNEY TO-MORROW

WIRELESS PROGRAMMES ON PAGE 19

DailyMirror

THE DAILY PICTURE PAPER WITH THE LARGEST NET SALE

No. 8,288   Registered at the G.P.O. as a Newspaper.   THURSDAY, JUNE 12, 1930   One Penny

£750 BALLOT COUPON TO-DAY

A NEW OCEAN GIANT

The Empress of Britain sliding towards the water at Clydebank, Glasgow.

MAN AND GIRL SHOT

Mr. Alfred Swaine.   Miss Mabel Jefferson.

These are the portraits of the victims of a shooting tragedy discovered at Bishop Wilton, Yorks, yesterday. The dead girl's father, a police sergeant, found their bodies while searching for the man, who was the son of a retired Army major. A double-barrel gun was lying nearby.—(" Daily Mirror " photo-telephony.)

CENTENARIAN LEARNS TYPING

Miss Julia Hadow, a Leamington resident aged 101, busy on her typewriter. An expert card player, she has now taken up typing as a further pastime. She is an excellent linguist and her energy is remarkable.

The Prince of Wales on the platform during the launching ceremony, which he performed yesterday, of the 42,000-ton liner Empress of Britain, owned by the Canadian Pacific Railway. Built for the Southampton-Quebec service, she will be the biggest ship operating between the two seaboards of the Empire, and is expected to create new records on the North Atlantic run.—(" Daily Mirror " photo-telephony.)

MACARTNEY ON TO-DAY'S TEST MATCH: SEE P. 3

WIRELESS PROGRAMMES ON PAGE 18

Daily Mirror

THE DAILY PICTURE   PAPER WITH THE LARGEST NET SALE

No. 8,289   Registered at the G.P.O. as a Newspaper.   FRIDAY, JUNE 13, 1930   One Penny

32 PAGES

THE PLAYERS FOR TO-DAY'S OPENING TEST

The English team will be selected from the above thirteen players. (A to B, standing) Duckworth, K. S. Duleepsinhji, R. W. V. Robins, Woolley, Tate, Tyldesley (R.), J. C. White, Hendren. (Sitting) Larwood, Hammond, A. P. F. Chapman, Hobbs and Sutcliffe. Duleepsinhji and Robins have not yet played against Australia in a Test match.

The Australian visitors. (A to B, standing) A. Jackson, S. McCabe, P. Hornibrook, A. Hurwood, T. Wall, E. a'Beckett, W. Ponsford, C. Grimmett, A. Kippax, C. W. Walker. (Sitting) A. Fairfax, V. Richardson, W. Woodfull (captain), Don Bradman and W. A. Oldfield, the wicket-keeper.

Cricket enthusiasts are crowding Nottingham for the first Test match, which begins to-day on the famous Trent Bridge ground. Weather experts promise long spells of sunshine, and only the fulfilment of this promise is needed to make the opening round for the Ashes a perfect festival of sport. Mr. C. G. Macartney, in a striking article on page 3, says that on paper England possesses the stronger team, and points out that only a few of the Australians have so far shown consistently good form.

ASCOT FASHIONS NUMBER: EXCLUSIVE PICTURES

DERBY FORECAST COMPETITION RESULT

Daily Mirror

THE DAILY PICTURE PAPER WITH THE LARGEST NET SALE

No. 8,291   Registered at the G.P.O. as a Newspaper.   MONDAY, JUNE 16, 1930   One Penny

£500 RACING CONTEST FORM

ELEGANT ASCOT

GREAT DAY FOR BRITAIN

A gown suitable for this week's Royal Ascot of mushroom-tinted satin with petal-shaped panels, worn with a coat of the same colour brocaded with gold. Baroque.—("Daily Mirror" photograph.) See also pages 12 and 13.

A general view of the game in progress during the Australian innings at Nottingham. Ponsford is seen during a dramatic moment puzzled by one of Tate's fizzers. The English bowler repeatedly broke through the Australian defence.

Leo Diegel and Abe Mitchell at St. Albans on Saturday, when the latter won his match against the American professional champion by 4 and 3.

(A to B) Mrs. Godfree and Mrs. Holcroft Watson, Britain, congratulated by Miss H. Jacobs and Mrs. Wills-Moody after the deciding match of the Wightman Cup regained from America at Wimbledon.

It was Britain's great day at cricket, tennis and golf on Saturday. In the Test match at Nottingham, at the close of play, Australia was 130 behind England's total of 270 with two wickets to fall. At Wimbledon the women of England won back the Wightman lawn tennis cup from U.S., and Abe Mitchell beat Leo Diegel, the U.S. professional, in their golf rubber match. See also page 24.

SECRET LONE FLIGHT PLANNED TO AMERICA

WIRELESS PROGRAMMES ON PAGE 19

DailyMirror

THE DAILY PICTURE PAPER WITH THE LARGEST NET SALE

No. 8,294   Registered at the G.P.O. as a Newspaper.   THURSDAY, JUNE 19, 1930   One Penny

ANOTHER CRICKET HINT BY MACARTNEY

TERRIFIC STORM STOPS RACING AT ASCOT

The King and Queen and Princess Mary, who are seen arriving at the course in the rain.

Hurrying to the course with umbrellas up to find shelter from the rain.

Mr. J. Dewar's The Macnab (F. Fox up) winning the Royal Hunt Cup from Grand Idol during a thunderstorm. The favourite, Lion Hearted, finished third. The winner started at 100 to 7.

Trying to keep cheerful in spite of the rain.

For the first time within living memory racing had to be abandoned at Ascot yesterday owing to a terrific thunderstorm accompanied by torrential rain, which broke soon after the finish of the Royal Hunt Cup. A bookmaker in Tattersall's Ring, Mr. Walter Holbein, of Southport, was struck by lightning and killed, while another man was injured.

Many of the spectators were soaked by the rain and long fashionable skirts were an impediment. The course and lawns were quickly converted into a swamp by the rain, which formed huge pools everywhere. The races which had to be abandoned will be divided between the programmes for to-day and to-morrow. See also pages 12 and 13.

MOMENTOUS PROPOSALS IN SIMON REPORT: P. 3

WIRELESS PROGRAMMES ON PAGE 17

DailyMirror

THE DAILY PICTURE PAPER WITH THE LARGEST NET SALE

No. 8,298   Registered at the G.P.O. as a Newspaper.   TUESDAY, JUNE 24, 1930   One Penny

£100 CROSSWORD PUZZLE

SEEDED WIMBLEDON PLAYER'S EARLY EXIT

G. Rogers, the Irish Davis Cup player, defeating H. Satoh, Japan, 1—6, 6—2, 6—3, 6—4.

W. Allison, the American, during his surprise winning match against E. F. Moon.

H. Cochet spinning his racket before his match against H. Timmer.

FRANCIS LORANG BROUGHT BACK TO LONDON

Francis Lorang, the financier (hand in pocket), with a detective, on arrival yesterday in London from France, where an extradition warrant was granted. Lorang was taken to Moor-lane Police Station, where he will be charged. He will appear at the Guildhall Court to-day.

Placing balls into an ice-cooler to preserve their even temperature. This innovation attracted much attention on the centre court.

The promise of thrills at the Wimbledon championships was borne out soon after the start yesterday when the seeded Australian, E. Moon, lost to W. Allison 6—1, 6—3, 6—3. And H. Timmer, Holland, won two sets off Cochet, the holder. The score was 6—4, 9—11, 4—6, 6—4, 6—2.

64

DRAMATIC NEW SERIAL BEGINS ON MONDAY

DailyMirror

THE DAILY PICTURE PAPER WITH THE LARGEST NET SALE

No. 8,299 | Registered at the G.P.O. as a Newspaper. | WEDNESDAY, JUNE 25, 1930 | One Penny

START OF IRELAND TO AMERICA FLIGHT

The Southern Cross surrounded by a considerable crowd at Portmarnock beach, near Dublin, yesterday, when it began an East-to-West Atlantic flight bid.

The crew—(A to B) Captain J. Saul, Irish; Major Kingsford-Smith, Australian; Mr. E. Van Dyk, Dutch; Mr. J. Stannage, South African.

Taxi-ing on the beach when on the point of leaving the ground.

The monoplane in the dim light of dawn. The start was made at 4.25 a.m.

Frequent reports were received by wireless from the Southern Cross after it had left the Irish coast, steamers in mid-Atlantic picking up some of the messages. Strong head winds lessened speed for a time and there was a perilous hour of blind flying through fog. Major Kingsford-Smith intends, if all goes well, to proceed to San Francisco, and so complete a round-the-world flight in his famous machine, having already crossed the Pacific and flown from Australia to Europe.—("Daily Mirror" photographs.)

65

NEW SERIAL, "OUTSIDE THE LAW," ON MONDAY

WIRELESS PROGRAMMES IN FULL ON PAGE 16

DailyMirror

THE DAILY PICTURE PAPER WITH THE LARGEST NET SALE

No. 8,302   Registered at the G.P.O. as a Newspaper.   SATURDAY, JUNE 28, 1930   One Penny

£1,000 RACING CONTEST

DULEEPSINHJI PLAYS—AND GETS A CENTURY

Richardson, in the slips, making a great effort to snap up a chance offered by Hammond.

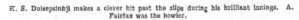

K. S. Duleepsinhji makes a clever hit past the slips during his brilliant innings. A. Fairfax was the bowler.

Hobbs and Woolley going out to bat. The choice of the latter as the great Surrey master's partner was a surprise to the spectators.

Oldfield, the Australian wicket-keeper, catching Hobbs off Fairfax's bowling.

The English captain—often called " Horseshoe Chapman "—once again won the toss, and England scored briskly on a perfect wicket at the opening of the second Test match at Lord's yesterday. With the exception of Hobbs, who was out for 1, all the leading batsmen collected runs at a good rate, with Duleepsinhji as the particular star. It was his first Test against Australia and he reached his century in three hours. Woolley scored 41 in forty-five minutes. See also page 20.

66

THE DAILY MIRROR, Wednesday, July 2, 1930.

ENGLAND CAPTAIN'S GREAT TEST MATCH INNINGS

WIRELESS PROGRAMMES ON PAGE 18

DailyMirror

THE DAILY PICTURE PAPER WITH THE LARGEST NET SALE

WIRELESS PROGRAMMES ON PAGE 18

No. 8,305   Registered at the G.P.O. as a Newspaper.   WEDNESDAY, JULY 2, 1930   One Penny

THE CLOSING THRILLS OF THE LOST TEST

A. P. F. Chapman, England's captain, hitting hard in his magnificent innings of 121.

W. M. Woodfull, Australia's captain, chaired after his team's victory by seven wickets.

A chance given to Hammond by A. F. Kippax.

Part of the crowd who called for the captains.

W. H. Ponsford at the wicket. He scored 14.

Although Australia won the Test match at Lord's yesterday with a second innings score of 72 for three wickets, three of their best batsmen, W. H. Ponsford, D. Bradman and A. F. Kippax, were dismissed for 22 runs. Bradman made only a single. In a brilliant stand A. P. F. Chapman flogged C. V. Grimmett's bowling for fours and sixes. He is the first English Test captain for twenty-five years to score a century. Scenes of wild enthusiasm marked the close of the match.

67

A TEST TEAM WHICH COULD <u>WIN</u> MATCHES: P. 2

WIRELESS PROGRAMMES ON PAGE 19

DailyMirror

THE DAILY PICTURE PAPER WITH THE LARGEST NET SALE

No. 8,306   Registered at the G.P.O. as a Newspaper.   THURSDAY, JULY 3, 1930   One Penny

ALL THE NEWS PICTURES

ALL-AMERICAN FINALS—GIRL STAR'S MISHAP

A fine picture of Mrs. Wills Moody, the women's singles holder, in play against Mme. Mathieu at Wimbledon yesterday. Mrs. Wills Moody won 6—3, 6—2.

Fraulein Aussem's collapse when she was playing Miss Ryan.

A portrait of Fraulein Aussem.

Ambulance men carrying Fraulein Aussem from the court.

One of the women's semi-finals at Wimbledon yesterday came to an abrupt end when Fraulein Cilli Aussem badly sprained her ankle and fainted. At the time she was level with her opponent, Miss Ryan, both having won two sets and four games. After Fraulein Aussem had been carried from the court the match was awarded to Miss Ryan, who will meet Mrs. Wills Moody in the final. Only Americans are left in both singles finals. See also page 24.

£750 ROAD SAFETY BALLOT: RESULT TO-DAY

ALL THE NEWS PICTURES

DailyMirror

THE DAILY PICTURE PAPER WITH THE LARGEST NET SALE

No. 8,308   Registered at the G.P.O. as a Newspaper.   SATURDAY, JULY 5, 1930   One Penny

BEST HOLIDAY INSURANCE

12 DEATHS IN EXPLOSION—500 HOMELESS

Doris Stark, aged five, who was injured by flying glass when she was returning home from school.

Firemen, protected from fumes, at work amid the ruins.

A scene of devastation at the factory, where there were about 300 people.—(" Daily Mirror " photo-telephony.)

A pigeon cote which was blown away by the explosion. Behind are some damaged windows.

Twelve men were killed and many people were injured when a fierce explosion wrecked chemical works yesterday at Castleford, Yorkshire. At least 300 houses were rendered uninhabitable and 500 people are without a roof. The town was shaken as if by an earthquake, and the roof of a school was blown off, three children being slightly hurt. Dense fumes from the factory made it impossible for rescuers to approach for some time. Many homeless people spent last night in schools.

MANY INSURANCE CLAIMS PAID: REGISTER NOW

WIRELESS PROGRAMMES ON PAGE 19

DailyMirror

THE DAILY PICTURE PAPER WITH THE LARGEST NET SALE

£100 CROSSWORD PUZZLE

No. 8,310   Registered at the G.P.O. as a Newspaper.   TUESDAY, JULY 8, 1930   One Penny

ROYAL OPENING OF AERODROME

VICTIM OF POST-BAG ROBBERY

Mr. William Hall, aged sixty, a postman of the West Central office, who was attacked by motor bandits yesterday and robbed of registered letters to the value of £2,000.—("Daily Mirror.")

Prince George speaking at the Handley Page test aerodrome which he opened yesterday at Radlett, Herts. In the background are a new forty-seater Handley Page machine and a pre-war monoplane.

SIR ARTHUR CONAN DOYLE DEAD

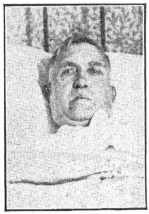

SUING TEACHER

Miss Mollie Frances Hunt, nineteen, of Guernsey, who is claiming damages from her former headmistress, Miss K. Damon, of Shanklin, I.W., for alleged libel and breach of duty.

Prince George greeting Mr. Handley Page on arrival at Radlett to open the aerodrome. Among the exhibitions witnessed by the Prince was wonderful trick flying by the Gugnunc machine.

Sir Arthur Conan Doyle, famous novelist and creator of Sherlock Holmes, who died at his home at Crowborough, Sussex, yesterday, in his seventy-second year. Lady Conan Doyle, who is seen with her husband, was with him at the end.

THE DAILY MIRROR, Thursday, July 10, 1930.

SIX BOYS DROWNED BATHING AT BLACKPOOL

WIRELESS PROGRAMMES ON PAGE 19

DailyMirror

THE DAILY PICTURE PAPER WITH THE LARGEST NET SALE

No. 8,312   Registered at the G.P.O. as a Newspaper.   THURSDAY, JULY 10, 1930   One Penny

LOMBARD THE BEST CITY GUIDE

AMERICAN HEIRESS'S BRILLIANT WEDDING

The gold quill pen carried on a white satin cushion by George Roblin, a page.

Bridesmaids and escorts leaving the church   Right the bride and bridegroom.

The bridesmaids waving to Mr. John Roland Robinson, a London barrister, and his bride, Miss Maysie Gasque, the twenty-year-old American heiress, at Stag-lane aerodrome last night, when the bridal couple left by air for the Continent. The marriage took place at St. Margaret's, Westminster. The twelve bridesmaids were representative of England, America, Italy, Germany and Russia. Two rings were placed on the bride's finger. The register was signed with a gold quill pen—an old Italian custom.

71

MEN FOR THE NEXT TEST XI: EXPERTS' CHOICE

LOMBARD THE BEST CITY GUIDE

DailyMirror

THE DAILY PICTURE PAPER WITH THE LARGEST NET SALE

No. 8,317   Registered at the G.P.O. as a Newspaper.   WEDNESDAY, JULY 16, 1930   One Penny

£500 RACING COUPON TO-DAY

FATAL RIOTING BY EGYPTIAN EXTREMISTS

Police in force to keep back a large crowd at Mansura, Egypt, where riots broke out on the occasion of the visit of Nahas Pasha, the Wafdist leader.

Rifles which were in action. Several of the police and public were killed.

Nahas Pasha (X) in a car surrounded by enthusiastic Wafdist supporters.

Special "Daily Mirror" pictures of the fatal rioting caused by Nahas Pasha's visit to Mansura. A sequel occurred yesterday at Alexandria when a strike demonstration in sympathy with the victims of the riot was made by Egyptian extremists. Seventeen people, including eight Europeans, were killed and 400 were injured. Order was restored only when the police fired on the mob from the roof of the Law Courts and charged with drawn batons. Reinforcements were sent from Cairo.

NEXT TEST TEAM: READERS' VIEWS—SEE PAGE 6

WIRELESS PROGRAMMES ON PAGE 17

DailyMirror

THE DAILY PICTURE PAPER WITH THE LARGEST NET SALE

No. 8,319 | Registered at the G.P.O. as a Newspaper. | FRIDAY, JULY 18, 1930 | One Penny

£500 RACING COUPON TO-DAY

SOCIALIST M.P. RUNS AWAY WITH THE MACE

Cromwell telling his soldiers to "take away this bauble" in 1653. The fifty-three members were driven from the House.—(From an engraving of the picture by Benjamin West, P.R.A.)

Sir Colin Keppel.

Mr. W. J. Brown.

Mr. F. N. Charrington, who renounced £1,250,000 to become a temperance reformer, standing in the Commons in 1915 after rushing in as a "stranger" and seizing the Mace as a protest against the M.P.s' bar. (Picture reproduced from the "Christian Herald.") Inset, a photograph of Mr. Charrington, who is now eighty.

Mr. John Beckett.

Mr. Fenner Brockway.

The gold Mace.

Mr. John Beckett (Socialist, Peckham) seized the Mace, the Commons symbol of authority, yesterday and ran with it down the floor of the House. He is the first person in the centuries-long life of Parliament to run away with the Mace. This disgraceful scene occurred when Mr. Beckett and Mr. W. J. Brown were tellers for the Noes in a division for the suspension of Mr. Fenner Brockway (Socialist, East Leyton). Shouting, "It is a damned disgrace," Mr. Beckett seized the Mace and, while other members gasped, ran towards the Bar of the House. The Mace was seized by Sir C. Keppel, the Serjeant-at-Arms. Mr. Brockway and Mr. Beckett were suspended.

BIG DEATH ROLL IN ITALIAN EARTHQUAKE

Daily Mirror

THE DAILY PICTURE ● PAPER WITH THE LARGEST NET SALE

No. 8,324 | Registered at the G.P.O. as a Newspaper. | THURSDAY, JULY 24, 1930 | One Penny

BRIDGE SWEPT AWAY IN YORKSHIRE FLOODS

Where Sleights Bridge over the River Esk, Yorkshire, was swept away by yesterday's floods, which followed a cloudburst. Whitby lifeboat was taken inland to assist victims.

The torrent which swept through Sleights. This town suffered most from the flood. In the village of Ruswarp the Whitby lifeboat rescued marooned inhabitants. Coastguards with rocket apparatus also rushed inland to rescue people whose homes were surrounded and in danger. At least one life was lost. In one case six people were rescued from the roof of an inn with the breeches buoy. Many roads were rendered impassable and trains had to be diverted. Whitby was partially cut off. See also page 20.

THE DUCHESS AT GLAMIS: EXCLUSIVE ARTICLE

£500 RACING COUPON

DailyMirror

THE DAILY PICTURE PAPER WITH THE LARGEST NET SALE

No. 8,325   Registered at the G.P.O. as a Newspaper.   FRIDAY, JULY 25, 1930   One Penny

MACARTNEY ON TO-DAY'S TEST

BUCKINGHAM PALACE GARDEN PARTY

The King (X) and the Queen with some of their six thousand visitors at the Royal Garden Party at Buckingham Palace yesterday afternoon. In spite of threatening clouds, there was little rain till late in the afternoon, and soon after three o'clock visitors began to arrive at the Palace gates. Gay flimsy frocks and wide-brimmed summer hats were worn by many of the women, and among the guests there were representatives of many nations and of all ranks of society. (See also page 14.)

THE DAILY MIRROR, Saturday, July 26, 1930.

MACARTNEY ON AUSTRALIA'S TEST MATCH FIGHT

£500
PICTURE
PUZZLE
WEEKLY

DailyMirror

THE DAILY PICTURE   PAPER WITH THE LARGEST NET SALE

No. 8,326   Registered at the G.P.O. as a Newspaper.   SATURDAY, JULY 26, 1930   One Penny

ALL
THE
NEWS
PICTURES

MID-ATLANTIC RESCUES FROM BURNING LINER

The last lifeboat being rowed from the burning Targis.

A lifeboat with rescued passengers and members of the Targis's crew.

Captain Frasie, captain of the Targis, and other officers.

The Targis after she had been abandoned. Everyone on board was saved.

The pictures above are the first to reach London of the rescue in mid-Atlantic of the passengers and crew of the North German Lloyd liner Targis, which caught fire 1,000 miles from the American coast. The British motor-liner Rangitata arrived at Southamp- ton last night with ten of the rescued passengers and fifty-three members of the crew who were picked up. They told thrilling stories of their escape in lifeboats and of the Rangitata's dash in response to S O S calls.

MR. SANDHAM ADMONISHED BY THE SPEAKER

DailyMirror

THE DAILY PICTURE PAPER WITH THE LARGEST NET SALE

No. 8,331 | Registered at the G.P.O. as a Newspaper. | FRIDAY, AUGUST 1, 1930 | One Penny

LADY ADARE'S APOLOGY

HOLIDAY EXODUS

Part of one of the huge queues at Waterloo Station yesterday, when many thousands left for the south coast.

£500,000 LOSSES

Viscountess Adare in London yesterday, when Judge Sir Alfred Tobin said to her at Westminster County Court: "I don't want you to go to prison. You have been guilty of grievous contempt of Court." A firm of antique dealers had a judgment summons for £24 against her. After admitting that she had torn up a writ, not knowing what it was, she apologised and paid the debt.

Sir Arthur Du Cros, chairman of the Parent Trust and Finance Company, Ltd., who has stated that he and his family lost nearly £500,000 through the Hatry crash.

The Premier with his daughter, Miss Ishbel MacDonald, just before leaving Victoria for the Continent. It is understood that he will see the Passion Play at Oberammergau.

WHEN OARS BECOME USELESS—CHOPPY SEAS CREATE DIFFICULTIES AT A REGATTA

Two volunteers coming to the assistance of one of the crews in the novice fours that was swamped at the Hastings and St. Leonards regatta yesterday.

MANY INSURANCE CLAIMS PAID: REGISTER NOW

ALL THE NEWS PICTURES

DailyMirror

THE DAILY PICTURE — PAPER WITH THE LARGEST NET SALE

No. 8,334 | Registered at the G.P.O. as a Newspaper. | TUESDAY, AUGUST 5, 1930 | One Penny

£100 CROSSWORD PUZZLE

TRIUMPHANT RETURN OF AMY JOHNSON

Amy Johnson, the air heroine of the Empire, on her dramatic arrival soon after s o'clock—some three hours late owing to a gale—at Croydon aerodrome yesterday evening. In the upper picture she is seen (marked with a cross) in front of the liner City of Glasgow, which brought her through terrific winds. Below, Miss Johnson is speaking to the crowd through microphones without showing a sign of nervousness. Behind her stands Lord Thomson, the Air Minister. Miss Bondfield, Minister of Labour, Sir Sefton Brancker and her parents were among those who greeted her. See also page 20.—("Daily Mirror" photographs.)

£500 RACING COMPETITION: RESULT ON PAGE 2

ALL THE NEWS PICTURES

DAILY Mirror
THE DAILY PICTURE PAPER WITH THE LARGEST NET SALE

No. 8,337 — Registered at the G.P.O. as a Newspaper. — FRIDAY, AUGUST 8, 1930 — One Penny

NEW SERIAL ON MONDAY

DOCTOR'S SON WEDS

Mr. Thomas Kemp, son of Dr. Kemp, of Nottingham, with his bride, Miss Nancie Sargent, daughter of Sir Percy Sargent, F.R.C.S., of Harley-street, after their wedding at All Souls Church, Langham-place, London, yesterday.

AIRSHIP ALIGHTS ON A LINER

Mr. Litchfield stepping from the deck into the airship, held down by sailors.

The Blimp Mayflower nearing the German liner Bremen in New York Harbour. It alighted on the deck to take off a passenger, Mr. P. W. Litchfield. The manœuvre was carried out without a hitch.

HONEYMOON STARTED 60 YEARS LATE

Mr. and Mrs. Grizzell, of Rotherhithe, greeted by Captain F. C. Cole, of the Crested Eagle, on which they went to Margate yesterday, their diamond wedding day, to start their honeymoon, for which they have never yet had time to get away.

READ C. G. MACARTNEY ON THE TEST ON MONDAY

WIRELESS PROGRAMMES IN FULL ON PAGE 16

DailyMirror

THE DAILY PICTURE PAPER WITH THE LARGEST NET SALE

No. 8,344   Registered at the G.P.O. as a Newspaper.   SATURDAY, AUGUST 16, 1930   One Penny

£500 PICTURE PUZZLE WEEKLY

EPSOM CRIME TURN   DECISIVE TEST BEGINS TO-DAY

Mr. John Hodson, who has stated to the police that he was in the company of a girl answering the description of Agnes Kesson, the murdered Epsom waitress, on Derby Day.

Getting ready the toss result board, which makes a chance prediction.

R. E. S. Wyatt, England's new captain, and Mr. H. Leveson-Gower talking at the Oval yesterday.

An aerial picture of the famous Oval ground where England, under the captaincy of R. E. S. Wyatt, meets Australia in the fifth and final Test match, beginning to-day. Every seat has been sold for the first four days, but unsettled weather conditions are forecast for the London area. Whysall (left), starting from an overnight score of 152, completed an innings of 248 for Notts against Northants at Trent Bridge yesterday. He is one of the fourteen players from whom the England side will be selected.

MACARTNEY ON ENGLAND'S COLLAPSE: SEE P. 3

SEE P. 3

WIRELESS PROGRAMMES IN FULL ON PAGE 16

DailyMirror

THE DAILY PICTURE PAPER WITH THE LARGEST NET SALE

SPECIAL EDITION

No. 8,346   Registered at the G.P.O. as a Newspaper.   TUESDAY, AUGUST 19, 1930   One Penny

BRADMAN NOW? AUSTRALIAN GIANTS FALL

W. H. Ponsford bowled by I. A. R. Peebles when his score stood at 110.

D. Bradman hitting I. A. R. Peebles. He and A. Kippax will continue batting to-day.

A way into the Oval through a fence.   The way out under police supervision.   Duckworth's dance after he had caught W. M. Woodfull off I. A. R. Peebles's bowling.

Australia made a determined reply yesterday to England's Test match score of 405 at the Oval, the first wicket stand by W. M. Woodfull and W. H. Ponsford yielding 159 runs. Ponsford scored his first Test century in England. At the close of play the score board showed 215 for two, of which Woodfull contributed 54. C. V. Grimmett has set up a record by taking twenty-eight wickets during the Test series. W. A. Oldfield did not allow a single bye during England's innings.

LONDON M.P. AND PARTY LOST IN YACHT WRECK

DailyMirror

THE DAILY PICTURE PAPER WITH THE LARGEST NET SALE

No. 8,349. Registered at the G.P.O. as a Newspaper. FRIDAY, AUGUST 22, 1930 One Penny

THE BABY PRINCESS SOUVENIR NUMBER

DAUGHTER BORN TO DUCHESS OF YORK

The Duchess of York, to whom a daughter was born yesterday at Glamis Castle, her ancestral home in the County of Angus, photographed with the Duke and their elder daughter, Princess Elizabeth. The whole Empire will welcome with joy the new Royal baby and wish it a long and happy life. The Duke of York is staying at the castle with the Earl and Countess of Strathmore, the Duchess's parents. Mr. J. R. Clynes was in attendance, as it is the duty of the Home Secretary to be present at the births of all who are in the direct line of succession to the Throne. No Royal child had been born in Scotland since Charles I, who first saw the light of day at Dunfermline in 1600.

MACARTNEY SUMS UP ON THE TESTS: PAGE 2

NEW £500 PUZZLE TO-DAY

DailyMirror
THE DAILY PICTURE PAPER WITH THE LARGEST NET SALE

No. 8,351   Registered at the G.P.O. as a Newspaper.   MONDAY, AUGUST 25, 1930   One Penny

READER WINS £250 PRIZE

FAMOUS DRIVERS CRASH IN BIG ROAD RACE

Captain A. C. R. Waite, of the Austin team, being congratulated by Sir H. Austin. Captain Waite's car skidded and toppled over.

Wreckage of Kaye Don's Alfa Romeo, which overturned and burst into flames. He had a rib broken, and was pulled clear only just in time.

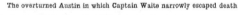

The overturned Austin in which Captain Waite narrowly escaped death.

Nuvolari, the winner, chaired by supporters. His average speed was 70.86 m.p.h., and that of Campari, who finished second, 70.76 m.p.h.

Competitors passing Captain Birkin's Bentley which skidded and dashed into a wall.

Rain fell most of the time during the Tourist Trophy race over the Ards Circuit in Ulster. The roads became treacherous despite the most careful preparation, and many accidents occurred. Kaye Don described his escape as the narrowest shave he remembered. About 250,000 spectators were spread round the thirteen-mile course, and they witnessed an Italian triumph. The first three cars were Alfa Romeos, with two English cars, an Alvis and an Austin, finishing fourth and fifth respectively. See also page 20.

THE DAILY MIRROR, Wednesday, August 27, 1930.

LONDON GETS HER HOTTEST DAY OF THE YEAR

Daily Mirror

THE DAILY PICTURE PAPER WITH THE LARGEST NET SALE

No. 8,353   Registered at the G.P.O. as a Newspaper.   WEDNESDAY AUGUST 27, 1930   One Penny

BATTLE SCENES ON THE INDIAN FRONTIER

A native lance-corporal shot in the arm.

Afridi attempting to rush the barbed wire in skirmishing order. They met with a hot reception.

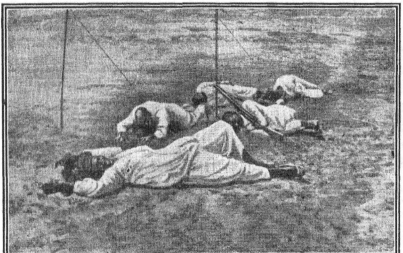

Dead and wounded after the battle. Only one Afridi got through the British wire entanglement.

The sentry sees the enemy on the horizon.

These exclusive "Daily Mirror" photographs, just received from India, give an excellent idea of the recent fighting between the Anglo-Indian troops and the Afridi on the North-West Frontier. At one time the Afridi actually penetrated the city of Peshawar, but were bombed by the R.A.F. and forced to withdraw to their mountain strongholds across the border. The revolt of the mountain tribes has now extended to Waziristan, where twenty-one British casualties have occurred on the Bannu-Kohat road.

DRUG ADDICT'S AMAZING STORY OF HIS LIFE

WIRELESS
PROGRAMMES
IN FULL
ON PAGE 16

DailyMirror

THE DAILY PICTURE PAPER WITH THE LARGEST NET SALE

SPECIAL
EDITION

No. 8,354 — Registered at the G.P.O. as a Newspaper. — THURSDAY, AUGUST 28, 1930 — One Penny

92 IN THE SHADE—BUT GETTING COOLER

Shopping in shorts in London—a sensible heat wave attire.

This was undoubtedly one of the coolest places in Brighton.

Many envied her as she walked at Willesden.

Japanese parasols and fountain spray in Trafalgar-square.

Business girls on holiday at Paignton dashing across Tor Bay in a powerful motor-boat.

Riviera summer weather has come to Southern England. Heat that is spreading from the Mediterranean made yesterday the hottest day of the year. Ninety-two degrees was registered at 4 p.m. at the Air Ministry. Only twice in ten years has this figure been exceeded. The great problem for city workers and holidaymakers was how to keep cool, and the second category naturally held an advantage. Cooler weather is forecast for to-day. See also pages 10 and 11.

94 IN THE SHADE IN LONDON YESTERDAY

WIRELESS PROGRAMMES ON PAGE 19

DailyMirror
THE DAILY PICTURE PAPER WITH THE LARGEST NET SALE

SPECIAL EDITION

No. 8,355   Registered at the G.P.O. as a Newspaper.   FRIDAY, AUGUST 29, 1930   One Penny

TWO BURNED TO DEATH AFTER ROAD SMASH

A motor-cycle and lorry after a smash followed by fire at London Colney, near St. Albans, yesterday. The motor-cyclist and pillion rider—Mr. and Mrs. J. H. James, of Birkenhead—were burned to death. Mr. James was wedged under the lorry and could not be reached until the brigade put out the flames.

FILM STAR'S TRIUMPHANT RETURN

Dorothy MacKaill, the Yorkshire-born Hollywood star, welcomed at Victoria last night. She had been absent from London for seven years. The daughter of a Hull newsagent, she was at one time a chorus girl in the West End.—("Daily Mirror" photograph.)

WOMAN SAVES CHILDREN

Mrs. Winifred Norton with the girls whom she rescued from drowning at Windsor. She plunged fully dressed into the Thames and finding the girls had disappeared dived to them and brought them ashore, one under each arm.

GASSED?

Mr. W. F. Forsyth, dental surgeon, found dead in his Portland-place surgery. Death is believed to have resulted from gas poisoning.

Mrs. Walker, who snatched her baby from her pram just before it was struck by the lorry. The child was uninjured.

NEW £500 PICTURE PUZZLE TO-DAY ON PAGE 23

DailyMirror

THE DAILY PICTURE — PAPER WITH THE LARGEST NET SALE

No. 8,357   Registered at the G.P.O. as a Newspaper.   MONDAY, SEPTEMBER 1, 1930   One Penny

THE KING AND QUEEN SEE NEW GRANDCHILD

Cheers for the King and Queen as they left Glamis Castle, Angus, for Balmoral, at the conclusion of an unexpected visit to see their new grandchild, daughter of the Duke and Duchess of York. A bulletin yesterday stated that the Duchess and the infant Princess were very well and that the child was gaining weight steadily.

WIDOW'S AEROPLANE SUICIDE

Captain Amlinger, a retired German Army officer, killed in an aeroplane accident in Russia, and his wife, aged twenty-two, who, because she could not face life without him, committed suicide by jumping from an aeroplane. The mystery of Captain Amlinger's presence in Russia raises grave military and political questions. The German Reichswehr Ministry at first stated that he was killed while riding.

The Queen at the Castle. She wore a beige coat and toque. The King was in Highland costume.

AS GANGSTER PASSED BY

The chief immigration officer leaving the liner Belgenland at Plymouth yesterday. Jack Diamond (inset), the notorious American gangster, was found to be on board, but he did not attempt to land. The liner proceeded to Antwerp.

THE DAILY MIRROR, Tuesday, September 2, 1930.

MANY INSURANCE CLAIMS PAID: REGISTER NOW

WIRELESS PROGRAMMES ON PAGE 17

DailyMirror

THE DAILY PICTURE PAPER WITH THE LARGEST NET SALE

SPECIAL EDITION

No. 8,358   Registered at the G.P.O. as a Newspaper.   TUESDAY, SEPTEMBER 2, 1930   One Penny

BROMLEY'S CHANCE TO-DAY

PRINCE FIRST ROYAL AIR MARSHAL

The Prince of Wales at Ballater yesterday. It was announced last night that the Prince has been promoted in all Services, and will be a Vice-Admiral, a Lieutenant-General and an Air-Marshal. He is the first member of the Royal Family to hold the rank of Air-Marshal. The King is Chief of the R.A.F.—(By "Daily Mirror" photo-telephony.)

Mr. V. C. Redwood speaking to bricklayers at Penge during his eve-of-poll tour yesterday.

START OF PARIS-NEW YORK NON-STOP FLIGHT ATTEMPT

The United Empire Party candidate in to-day's by-election at Bromley, Kent, answering voters' questions by telephone. By returning him to Parliament the electors will help to bring prosperity back to Britain.—("Daily Mirror" photographs.)

The aeroplane Question Mark, in which Captain Costes and M. Bellonte set out yesterday morning on an attempted flight to New York, photographed over Le Bourget just after the start. (Inset) Mme. Costes, a Russian Princess by birth saying good-bye to her husband. Weather conditions were stated to be ideal over the Atlantic.

88

THE DAILY MIRROR. Friday, September 5, 1930.

SCHNEIDER RACE AIRMAN IN £12,800 CHARGE

WIRELESS PROGRAMMES ON PAGE 19

DailyMirror

THE DAILY PICTURE PAPER WITH THE LARGEST NET SALE

No. 8,361   Registered at the G.P.O. as a Newspaper.   FRIDAY, SEPTEMBER 5, 1930   One Penny

£500 RACING COUPON TO-DAY

ARMY AND NAVY MANOEUVRES: AN 'INVASION'

The handymen of the Navy are seen superintending the landing of a tank on the beach at Newton Bay, Isle of Wight.

The Nightland Army landing by the aid of the Navy on an imaginary island possession where "war" rages.

Admiral of the Fleet Sir Roger Keyes and Lieutenant-General Sir A. A. Montgomery-Massingberd watching the progress of the "invasion."

Active naval and military manœuvres by Nightland, based at Portsmouth, and Dayland, in the Isle of Wight, are now in progress.

SPECIAL TRAIN FOR BABY

Mrs. S. Headley with her three-months-old baby, whom she left behind at Goole Station owing to the unexpected departure of a train. The child was taken after its mother in another train and restored to her.

WELL-KNOWN GIRL GOLFER WEDS

Mr. Alan Hickman assisting his bride, Miss Kitty Beard, the Dorset golf champion, to cut the wedding cake after their wedding at the Church of the Holy Trinity, Brompton, S.W., yesterday.

THE DAILY MIRROR. Saturday, September 6, 1930.

£500 RACING CONTEST RESULT TO-DAY ON P. 2

WIRELESS PROGRAMMES IN FULL ON PAGE 16

DailyMirror

THE DAILY PICTURE PAPER WITH THE LARGEST NET SALE

No. 8,362   Registered at the G.P.O. as a Newspaper.   SATURDAY, SEPTEMBER 6, 1930   One Penny

LAUGH DAILY WITH THE PATER

FATAL HARBOUR CRANE CRASH | SHOT IN HUT

An overturned crane at Shoreham Harbour yesterday. It overbalanced while lifting a heavy load of timber during repair work. The driver, Mr. A. G. S. Streeter, was killed and Mr. Samuel Kittle seriously injured.

Mr. Robert Baxter, a sales manager and traveller, of Greenwich, who was yesterday found injured by a revolver shot in a hut near Le Touquet. He told the police that it was an accident. Doctors hope to save his life. He is thirty-nine years of age.— ("Daily Mirror" photograph.)

SOCIETY ROMANCE

Miss Margaret Duveen, the niece of Sir Joseph Duveen, the world-famous art dealer, who is to wed Mr. Harry Grayson, of Sutherland-street, S.W., a riding-master. She is twenty-two.

HEAVY DEATH ROLL IN WEST INDIES CYCLONE DISASTER

A main business street of Santo Domingo, in the West Indies, which has been devastated by a cyclone. Over 1,000 inhabitants are reported dead and about 30,000 have, it is estimated, been rendered homeless. There is a grave shortage of food and water, but aid is being rushed to the stricken district from U.S.A. The hurricane is sweeping towards Florida.

THE DAILY MIRROR, Thursday, September 11, 1930.

POISONED SWEETS: FURTHER DEVELOPMENTS

WIRELESS PROGRAMMES ON PAGE 17

DailyMirror

THE DAILY PICTURE PAPER WITH THE LARGEST NET SALE

LOMBARD THE BEST CITY GUIDE

No. 8,366   Registered at the G.P.O. as a Newspaper.   THURSDAY, SEPTEMBER 11, 1930   One Penny

SINGAPORE'S ST. LEGER VICTORY

The finish of the race for the St. Leger Stakes. Singapore and Lord Woolavington's Parenthesis were both equal favourites at four to one.

TEST PLAYER FOUND DEAD

Major G. A. Faulkner, the famous South African cricketer, found dead yesterday in a gas-filled room at the Faulkner School of Cricket, Walham Green. He played both for South Africa and England.

Lord Glanely leading in his Singapore after it had won the St. Leger by one and a half lengths from Parenthesis at Doncaster yesterday.—("Daily Mirror.")

NINETEEN-YEAR-OLD GIRL SWIMS THE CHANNEL

Miss Peggy Duncan, a nineteen-year-old South African, after she had swum the Channel from Cape Gris-Nez to the South Foreland cliffs in 15h. 17m. She holds a message given to her by the Mayor of Boulogne for the Mayor of Dover. Inset, Miss Duncan nearing land.

MANY MORE READERS' DEATH CLAIMS PAID

DailyMirror

THE DAILY PICTURE PAPER WITH THE LARGEST NET SALE

No. 8,370   Registered at the G.P.O. as a Newspaper.   TUESDAY, SEPTEMBER 16, 1930   One Penny

GERMAN FASCISTS' GREAT ELECTION SUCCESS

Police searching Nationalist supporters for arms in Berlin, during the German General Elections, the results of which were announced yesterday. The National Socialist party or German Fascists, who favour a dictatorship, have had astonishing success, winning 107 seats as against twelve in the old Reichstag. The Communists have increased their vote.

Herr Adolf Hitler, the National Socialists' leader. As an Austrian he cannot be a Reichstag candidate.

BABY HEIR DIES

Lady Weymouth, wife of Viscount Weymouth, whose infant son and heir, the Hon. Thomas Timothy Thynne has died. The baby was born last October. They have a daughter.

U.S. GIRL TWINS' CHANNEL SWIM

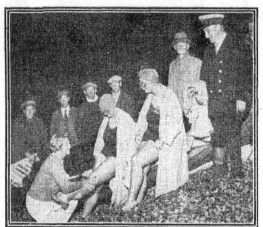

Phyllis and Berenice, the American Zitenfeld twins, being greased by their mother before starting from the South Foreland on an attempt to swim the Channel. They fought pluckily against unfavourable weather conditions.

M.P. HELD UP

Professor P. J. Noel Baker, M.P., held up by an armed burglar in his hotel bedroom at Geneva, where he is a delegate to the League Assembly. His wife was with him.

BOY SUSPECT

Andre Leloutre, recognised yesterday as having been present at the scene of the murder at Mrs. Wilson on the day the crime was committed.

EPSOM CRIME INQUEST: FRESH SENSATIONS

Daily Mirror

THE DAILY PICTURE PAPER WITH THE LARGEST NET SALE

No. 8,371   Registered at the G.P.O. as a Newspaper.   WEDNESDAY, SEPTEMBER 17, 1930   One Penny

A MILLIONAIRE'S ROMANCE

EPSOM VERDICT

Mr. Reginald Cory, the Welsh millionaire.

AGATHA CHRISTIE WEDS

Mrs. Agatha Christie, the writer of mystery novels, whose disappearance four years ago caused a great sensation, and her bridegroom, Mr. Max E. L. Mallowan. They were married secretly at Edinburgh.

Miss Rosa Blanche Kester, of Cambridge, whose marriage to Mr. Reginald Cory, colliery owner and shipping magnate, of Duffryn, near Cardiff, was revealed yesterday. She had been employed at a bookshop for six years. The wedding took place about a fortnight ago.

Mr. F. W. Deats.

Agnes Kesson, the victim.

Mr. J. W. Hodson, a witness.

That Agnes Kesson was strangled, but that there was insufficient evidence to state by whom, was the jury's verdict at the Epsom murder inquest yesterday. Mr. J. W. Hodson, of Waterloo-road, S.E., gave dramatic evidence. He identified Mr. F. W. Deats, the dead girl's employer, as the man whom he said he saw on Derby Day seize the arm of a girl he believed to be Agnes Kesson and take her away in a car.

NEW SERIAL, "MAELSTROM," BEGINS ON PAGE 17

£300 RADIO CONTEST

DailyMirror

THE DAILY PICTURE PAPER WITH THE LARGEST NET SALE

No. 8,375   Registered at the G.P.O. as a Newspaper.   MONDAY, SEPTEMBER 22, 1930   One Penny

NEW £500 PUZZLE TO-DAY

WEDDING AT THE TOWER OF LONDON

Mr. Percy Hatton with his bride, Miss Lillian Smoker, after marriage at the Tower of London. With them is the bride's father, the Chief Warder.—("Daily Mirror.")

DUKE'S INSPECTION OF CADETS

The Duke of Connaught greeting officers of the Royal Military College, Sandhurst, before church parade yesterday, when he inspected the cadets of the college. Watching him from the dais is Princess Ingrid of Sweden (X), his granddaughter.

FURY OF THE GREAT WEEK-END GALE

The bed on which the roof of a house at Netherton, Worcestershire, collapsed during the gale. A woman of seventy-two was seriously injured. Right, taking hurried refuge from a wave on Hastings front yesterday. The week-end gale caused Channel shipwrecks and delay to even Atlantic liners, and on land heavy rain did damage to crops and caused flooding. At Folkestone the wind velocity reached 83 m.p.h. Two thousand holiday-makers were held up in Jersey by the weather.—("Daily Mirror.")

BEGIN READING "MAELSTROM" ON PAGE 13

DailyMirror

THE DAILY PICTURE PAPER WITH THE LARGEST NET SALE

No. 8,376 Registered at the G.P.O. as a Newspaper. TUESDAY, SEPTEMBER 23, 1930 One Penny

5 DEATHS IN AIR STUNTS

ACTOR ON TRIAL

Neil McKay (Neil McNeil Walker), the Scottish comedian, who is on trial with another man at the Old Bailey on a serious charge arising from allegations made by Miss Ivy Braham (right), a dancer.

FOR THE ROUND TABLE CONFERENCE

Vadine Stachevski entering an aeroplane for a demonstration with three parachutes near Brussels. He cut away two parachutes after falling 500 feet with each, but the third failed to open and he was killed.

Herr Schindler performing an acrobatic feat at Berlin, and aeroplanes in collision during stunts in which he and three other airmen were killed over Boblingen aerodrome, near Stuttgart. Just before the collision Schindler was climbing from one 'plane up a rope ladder to another, but he lost his hold and fell to earth. When the 'planes crashed one pilot made an unsuccessful jump with a parachute.

Sir Muhammad Shafi, a leading Moslem politician and lawyer in the Punjab, and his daughter, Mrs. Shah Nawaz, on arrival in London last night. They are delegates to the Indian and Imperial Conferences.

NEW £500 RACING COMPETITION STARTS TO-DAY

FIRST RADIO CONTEST RESULT

DailyMirror

THE DAILY PICTURE PAPER WITH THE LARGEST NET SALE

No. 8,379   Registered at the G.P.O. as a Newspaper.   FRIDAY, SEPTEMBER 26, 1930   One Penny

28 PAGES

"HEADS WILL ROLL IN THE SAND"—HITLER

The trial scene. The officers are accused of treasonable activities in Hitler's party's interests.

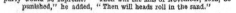

Herr Hitler (nearer camera) giving evidence, and Herr Laubin, one of the accused officers at the trial.

Great sensation was caused by Herr Adolf Hitler, the German Fascists' or National Socialists' leader, at the trial of three officers in Leipzig yesterday when he declared that in a few more elections his party would be supreme. "Then will the sins of November, 1918, be punished," he added, "Then will heads roll in the sand."

ATTEMPTED ASSASSINATION ECHO

De Rosa (X), the Italian anti-Fascist, at his trial in Brussels. He is accused of attempting to assassinate the Italian Crown Prince during the Prince's visit to Brussels for his betrothal to Princess Marie Jose

TO TAKE THE VEIL

Mlle. Yvonne Hautin, aged twenty-nine, an actress of the Paris Comedie Francaise company, who has decided to become a nun. A brilliant stage career had been prophesied for her. She is to enter a Benedictine Convent and will eventually take final vows.

EX-MAHARAJAH'S DAUGHTER

Raji Sharda, the infant daughter of Sir Tuko Ji Rao, ex-Maharajah of Indore, with her mother the Maharani Devi Smar Mistha, formerly an American girl, Miss Nancy Miller, who married the ex-Maharajah in 1928. The baby recently sailed for England with her parents.

MANY INSURANCE CLAIMS PAID: REGISTER NOW

DailyMirror

THE DAILY PICTURE PAPER WITH THE LARGEST NET SALE

No. 8,388 — Registered at the G.P.O. as a Newspaper. — TUESDAY, OCTOBER 7, 1930 — One Penny

SIR J. SALMOND EXAMINES R 101 WRECKAGE

Sir John Salmond greeting the Mayor of Allonne.

General Barres, of the French Air Force, showing two watches found in the debris to Sir John Salmond.

Air Chief Marshal Sir John Salmond inspecting the wreckage of R 101.

Stooping to examine a fragment of debris. Sir John flew to the scene of the disaster.

Sir John Salmond, Chief of the Air Staff, who flew to the scene of the R 101 disaster at Allonne, attended a meeting of the Air Council yesterday. To-day has been decreed a day of national mourning in France by M. Tardieu. He will be present at a solemn service held in Beauvais Cathedral before the departure of the bodies of the victims. They will be taken to Dover by the destroyers Tempest and Tribune. Air-Commodore F. V. Holt said yesterday that the French authorities state that forty-seven bodies have been found. He added that if this is true there must have been a stowaway on board the airship. See also pages 5, 14, 15 and 28.

THE DAILY MIRROR, Saturday, October 11, 1930.

THE EMPIRE'S HOMAGE TO R 101 DEAD

DailyMirror

THE DAILY PICTURE PAPER WITH THE LARGEST NET SALE

No. 8,392   Registered at the G.P.O. as a Newspaper.   SATURDAY, OCTOBER 11, 1930   One Penny

LYING·IN·STATE
NUMBER
IMPRESSIVE SCENES

NIGH THEIR JOURNEY'S END

THE LYING-IN-STATE IN WESTMINSTER'S ANCIENT HALL

A " Daily Mirror " picture of the sad and impressive scene in historic Westminster Hall yesterday when the coffins of the forty-eight men killed in the R 101 disaster lay in honoured state. An officer and men of the R.A.F., the latter with arms reversed, kept motionless guard beside the biers, around which were hundreds of beautiful wreaths, with that sent by the King and Queen at the head. An endless stream of people, numbering many thousands, passed in silent homage through the dimly-lit hall and paused reverently around the coffins, each of which was covered with the Union Jack. The coffins will be borne in procession through London this morning. See pages 5, 12, 13, 20 and 24.

£500 RACING FORECAST ENTRY COUPON DAILY

WIRELESS PROGRAMMES ON PAGE 23

DailyMirror
THE DAILY PICTURE PAPER WITH THE LARGEST NET SALE

No. 8,396   Registered at the G.P.O. as a Newspaper.   THURSDAY, OCTOBER 16, 1930   One Penny

SPECIAL EDITION

R101 SURVIVORS COME HOME

COUSIN OF THE DUCHESS OF YORK TO MARRY

Miss Pamela Bowes-Lyon, a cousin of the Duchess of York, and—

Three of the six survivors of the R101 disaster on arrival at Croydon yesterday by aeroplane from Beauvais. V. Savory, engineer (tallest), A. J. Cook, engineer (centre) and A. Disley, wireless operator. Cook was taken to hospital.—("Daily Mirror.")

CESAREWITCH WON BY THE AGA KHAN

INDIA ARREST

Mr. K. F. Nariman, Swarajist leader and president of the Bombay League of Youth, arrested yesterday, was sentenced to six months' simple imprisonment.

The Aga Khan, owner of Ut Majeur.

Ut Majeur and M. Beary, who rode it to victory yesterday.

Ut Majeur brought the Aga Khan his second Cesarewitch victory yesterday by winning the famous race in a canter. The Aga Khan now heads the winning owners' list.

—her fiancé, Pilot-Officer Lord Malcolm Douglas-Hamilton, the third son of the Duke and Duchess of Hamilton and Brandon. Their engagement was announced yesterday. Both are twenty-one years of age.

99

THE DAILY MIRROR, Friday, October 17, 1930.

FEATURES OF THE MOTOR SHOW: PICTURES

WIRELESS PROGRAMMES ON PAGE 23

DailyMirror

THE DAILY PICTURE PAPER WITH THE LARGEST NET SALE

28 PAGES

No. 8,397. Registered at the G.P.O. as a Newspaper. FRIDAY, OCTOBER 17, 1930 One Penny

WORLD'S GREATEST AIR RACE

Port Darwin, the goal of both airmen.

Wing-Commander Kingsford Smith and Flight-Lieutenant Hill, both attempting to beat Hinkler's England-to-Australia flight record, are the heroes of the greatest air duel in history. Hill may land at Port Darwin to-day, but his progress has been eclipsed by Kingsford Smith, who left London four days after him and reached Singapore yesterday, five days ahead of Hinkler's time.

Wing-Commander Kingsford Smith, conqueror of Atlantic and Pacific.

Flight-Lieutenant C. W. Hill, of Henlow.

DUKE LEAVES FOR ABYSSINIA FOR EMPEROR'S CORONATION

The Prince of Wales and the Duke of Gloucester at Victoria Station yesterday when the Duke left for Abyssinia to represent the King at the coronation on November 2 of Ras Tafari as Emperor of Ethiopia.

NEW £500 PICTURE PUZZLE TO-DAY: PAGE 27

WIRELESS PROGRAMMES ON PAGE 19

DailyMirror
THE DAILY PICTURE PAPER WITH THE LARGEST NET SALE

READER WINS £250 PRIZE

No. 8,399   Registered at the G.P.O. as a Newspaper.   MONDAY, OCTOBER 20, 1930   One Penny

KINGSFORD SMITH'S AMAZING AIR RECORD

Flight-Lieutenant Hill, who was ahead of Kingsford Smith, but damaged his machine on the last lap.

Wing-Commander Kingsford Smith with his father and mother. He left England on October 9, reaching Port Darwin early yesterday morning.

Flt.-Lieutenant Worsley, of 29th R.A.F. Squadron.

Captain Bert Hinkler, who immediately telegraphed congratulations to Wing-Commander Kingsford Smith on breaking his record.

SCHNEIDER PILOT KILLED

The wrecked car of Flight-Lieutenant O. E. Worsley, who died in Windsor Hospital following a collision on the Great Bath Road near Slough. He was a member of the victorious British Schneider Trophy team in 1927 at Venice.

The Southern Cross Junior, in which Kingsford Smith (in cockpit) reached Port Darwin early yesterday. He has set up the record time of 10 days 2 hours 10 minutes for a flight from England to Australia, beating Hinkler's time by over five days.

THE DAILY MIRROR, Wednesday, October 22, 1930.

100 DEAD IN GERMAN MINE DISASTER: PAGE 3

DailyMirror

THE DAILY PICTURE PAPER WITH THE LARGEST NET SALE

No. 8,401   Registered at the G.P.O. as a Newspaper.   WEDNESDAY, OCTOBER 22, 1930   One Penny

PRINCE OF WALES AMONG THE FISHER GIRLS

Cutting the ribbon to open the Haven Bridge.

The Prince of Wales interested in the cleaning of fish by a number of Scottish fisher girls during his visit to Yarmouth yesterday.

NEW PRINCESS HOME

Princess Margaret, the baby daughter of the Duke and Duchess of York, leaving 145, Piccadilly for her first drive in London yesterday afternoon. She arrived early in the morning with her father and mother.

The procession from the £200,000 Haven Bridge after it had been opened yesterday by the Prince of Wales. Thousands of Scottish fisher girls crowded round the Prince, formed a procession behind him, and cheered and sang. He went on board a herring trawler laden with a night's catch. See also pages 12 and 13.—(" Daily Mirror " photographs.)

WHAT IS WRONG WITH OUR DOCTORS? PAGE 2

WIRELESS PROGRAMMES ON PAGE 19

Daily Mirror
THE DAILY PICTURE PAPER WITH THE LARGEST NET SALE

No. 8,402   Registered at the G.P.O. as a Newspaper.   THURSDAY, OCTOBER 23, 1930   One Penny

GRAMOPHONE ARTICLE TO-DAY

OVER 250 DEAD IN MINE DISASTER

Shattered remains of buildings and machinery at Alsdorf pithead.

FAMOUS LAWYER HEADS R101 DISASTER INQUIRY

Sir John Simon.   Professor C. E. Inglis.   Lieut.-Col. Moore-Brabazon.

It was announced last night that the Court of Inquiry into the R101 disaster will consist of Sir John Simon, the famous legal authority, sitting with Lieutenant-Colonel Moore-Brabazon and Professor C. E. Inglis, Cambridge Professor of Mechanism and Applied Mechanics, acting as assessors.

Carrying an injured survivor of the explosion to hospital. The known death-roll increased yesterday to over 250. This will, it is feared, be yet greater, as many miners are still entombed. Almost every household in Alsdorf has suffered bereavement. Rescue parties yesterday received signals from trapped survivors. See also page 13.

THE DAILY MIRROR, Tuesday, October 28, 1930

MANY MORE INSURANCE CLAIMS PAID TO-DAY

Daily Mirror

THE DAILY PICTURE PAPER WITH THE LARGEST NET SALE

No. 8,406 | Registered at the G.P.O. as a Newspaper. | TUESDAY, OCTOBER 28, 1930 | One Penny

PRINCESS MARGARET—FIRST PICTURE

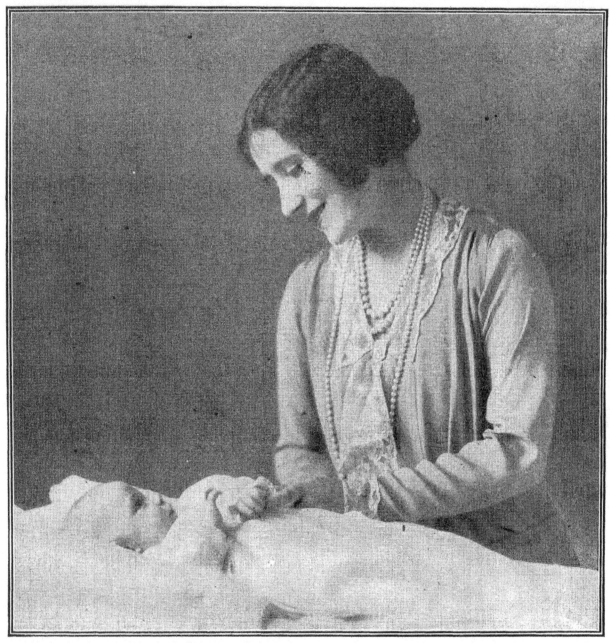

The Duchess of York with her second daughter, Princess Margaret Rose of York, the fourth grandchild of the King and Queen. A happy and contented baby, Princess Margaret has endeared herself to all visitors to her parents' Piccadilly home, whither she was brought with her little sister, Princess Elizabeth, from Glamis Castle to await her christening on Thursday in the private chapel of Buckingham Palace. This and other pictures on pages 12 and 13 are the first photographs of the baby Princess.

DELIGHTFUL NEW SERIAL BEGINS ON MONDAY

WIRELESS PROGRAMMES ON PAGE 19

DailyMirror

THE DAILY PICTURE — PAPER WITH THE LARGEST NET SALE

No. 8,407 — Registered at the G.P.O. as a Newspaper. — WEDNESDAY, OCTOBER 29, 1930 — One Penny

£500 RACING COUPON DAILY

BISHOP'S DEATH NEAR PARLIAMENT

DISCLOSURES AT R 101 INQUIRY

The Bishop of Worcester, Dr. E. H. Pearce, who collapsed and died in a few minutes in Parliament-square yesterday when walking with a friend to attend the opening of Parliament.

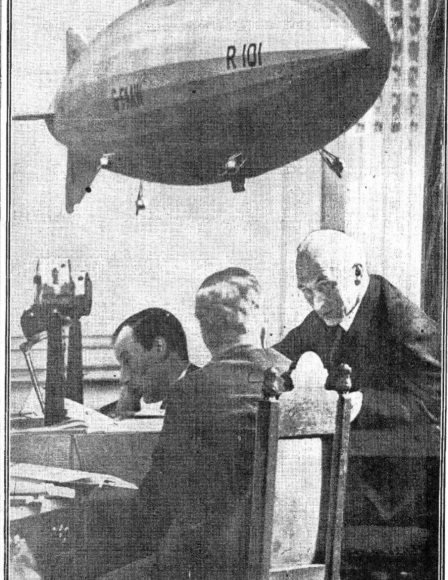

Sir William Jowitt, the Attorney-General, speaking at the R 101 inquiry which opened yesterday at the Institute of Civil Engineers, Westminster. Right: Sir John Simon, the president, sitting between Lieutenant-Colonel Moore-Brabazon (profile) and Professor Inglis, the assessors. Above is a model of the airship. The Attorney-General made important disclosures. He said that he believed the flight began when it did because Lord Thomson wanted it to take place during the Imperial Conference.

COMPLETE SHORT STORY TO-DAY ON PAGE 15

WIRELESS PROGRAMMES ON PAGE 23

DailyMirror
THE DAILY PICTURE — PAPER WITH THE LARGEST NET SALE

No. 8,408   Registered at the G.P.O. as a Newspaper.   THURSDAY, OCTOBER 30, 1930   One Penny

NEW SERIAL ON MONDAY

CAMBRIDGESHIRE WINNER AT 50-1

The finish of the Cambridgeshire, won by The Pen (x), a 50 to 1 starter, at Newmarket yesterday. Inset, Mrs. Hartigan, owner of The Pen, which, ridden by C. Richards, beat Racedale by a head. Two backers have each won £3,011 8s. for their 10s. stakes in the tote double on the Cesarewitch and Cambridgeshire. See also page 12.—("Daily Mirror" photograph.)

MORE R 101 REVELATIONS BY ATTORNEY-GENERAL

Mrs. Irwin, widow of Flight-Lieutenant H. C. Irwin, A.F.C., captain of R 101, leaving the inquiry yesterday. Sir W. Jowitt, the Attorney-General (tallest) made further revelations. He stated that it was clear that R 101's short trial flight was unsatisfactory. The captain of the R 100 took that view.

DEATH PUZZLE

Mr. Hubert Booty, who died at Hove. He alleged he had been drugged and robbed in London. The police are trying to trace authors of anonymous messages sent him.

WEDS AT 97

Mr. John Graham, coroner of Chester Ward of Durham, who was married yesterday in Upper Norwood, S.E., to Miss E. Ashton. He is 97 she is nearly 70.

GREAT NEW SERIAL BEGINS TO-DAY: PAGE 15

DailyMirror

THE DAILY PICTURE PAPER WITH THE LARGEST NET SALE

No. 8,411 | Registered at the G.P.O. as a Newspaper. | MONDAY, NOVEMBER 3, 1930 | One Penny

EMPIRE CHIEFS SEE MIMIC NAVAL BATTLE

Destroyers screening Nelson, from which statesmen of the Empire and delegates to the Indian Round Table Conference witnessed a naval display off Portland.

Warships taking part in the manœuvres. Inset (A to B) Mr. A. V. Alexander, First Lord of the Admiralty, Admiral Sir M. Hodges, Commander-in-Chief of the Atlantic Fleet, Mr. R. B. Bennett, Canadian Premier, Mr. J. H. Thomas, and Mr. G. W. Forbes, New Zealand Premier, on board the Nelson. This battleship was attacked by submarines and subjected to torpedo fire during the mimic battle. Escorted by flying-boats, she cut her way through a minefield after rigging a paravane.

DO NOT MISS OUR BRILLIANT NEW SERIAL: PAGE 15

WIRELESS PROGRAMMES ON PAGE 23

Daily Mirror

THE DAILY PICTURE PAPER WITH THE LARGEST NET SALE

SPECIAL EDITION

No. 8,412   Registered at the G.P.O. as a Newspaper.   TUESDAY, NOVEMBER 4, 1930   One Penny

OPENING OF THE HUNTING SEASON

DOCTOR DROWNED DURING GALE

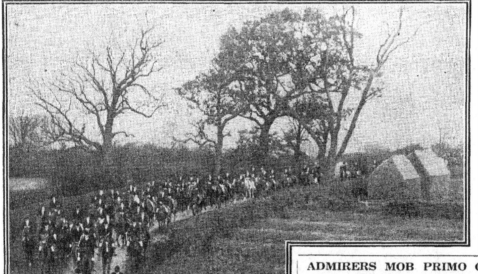

Dr. Cecil Watts, of Shenfield, Essex, a house surgeon at St. Bartholomew's Hospital, drowned when he slipped and fell overboard from a cutter in the Channel during a gale.

ADMIRERS MOB PRIMO CARNERA IN ROME

The pack leading the field to the covert side at Gartree Hill after the meet of the Quorn Foxhounds at Kirbygate, near Melton Mowbray, yesterday. It marked the official opening of the hunting season. See also page 12.

Primo Carnera, the giant Italian boxer, in the centre of a surging mass of enthusiasts outside the station on his arrival in Rome. He has telegraphed to Signor Mussolini asking to be enrolled in a Black Shirt (Fascist) battalion.

THE DAILY MIRROR, Thursday, November 6, 1930.

SIR JOHN SIMON AGAINST THE GOVERNMENT

WIRELESS PROGRAMMES ON PAGE 19

Daily Mirror

THE DAILY PICTURE PAPER WITH THE LARGEST NET SALE

No. 8,414   Registered at the G.P.O. as a Newspaper.   THURSDAY, NOVEMBER 6, 1930   One Penny

GUGNUNC XMAS GIFT FUND

AWARDED £800 AGAINST LADY EVES

ENGLISH TENNIS STAR'S DEATH

Mrs. Rhoda Elizabeth Flanders, to whom damages of £800 for slander and £5 for assault were awarded yesterday against Sir Charles and Lady Eves. The action followed the boarding of Lady Eves's dogs at Mrs. Flanders's kennels.

As lawn tennis enthusiasts knew her, remarkably active and agile.

A studio portrait of Mrs. Munro.

EXPLOSION OF THE GUY AS CLIMAX OF GREAT BONFIRE

A superb Guy set up by the Lingfield, Surrey, Bonfire Club, watched by thousands last night as flames flickered round its boots. Its end (shown inset) was truly dazzling. Many bonfire clubs have lately been revived.—("Daily Mirror.")

Mrs. Hamish Munro, formerly Miss Evelyn Colyer, whose death at Bishnauth, Assam, was announced last night, photographed with her husband, a tea planter. Twins were born to her a week ago. She twice reached the women's doubles final at Wimbledon.

THE DAILY MIRROR, Monday, November 10, 1930.

£1,000 OFFERED IN PRIZES FOR READERS TO-DAY

NEW SPORT FEATURE PAGE 27

DailyMirror

THE DAILY PICTURE PAPER WITH THE LARGEST NET SALE

No. 8,417 — Registered at the G.P.O. as a Newspaper. — MONDAY, NOVEMBER 10, 1930 — One Penny

PICTURE PUZZLE ON PAGE 22 TO-DAY

3,000 EX-SERVICE JEWS AT ARMISTICE PARADE

General Sir Ian Hamilton and Lieutenant-Colonel C. S. Myers, president of the Jewish National Armistice Service, with Jewish women who served as nurses during the war.

The Chief Rabbi and Rabbi Dayan M. Gollop conducting the service. Seated between Sir Ian Hamilton (silk hat) and Lieutenant Keysor, V.C., is Major J. B. Cohen, M.P.

The Armistice parade of ex-Service Jews from many parts of Britain on Horse Guards Parade yesterday. Over 3,000 attended, and after being inspected by General Sir Ian Hamilton they marched past the Cenotaph, where a wreath was placed by Lieutenant L. Keysor, V.C., and Private Jack White, V.C. The march was continued to the Horse Guards for a service, conducted by Dr. J. H. Hertz, Chief Rabbi, and Rabbi Dayan M. Gollop, senior Jewish Chaplain to the Forces. See page 28.

ARMISTICE DAY NUMBER TO-MORROW:

PAGES OF PICTURES

£100 CROSSWORD PUZZLE

Daily Mirror

THE DAILY PICTURE PAPER WITH THE LARGEST NET SALE

No. 8,418   Registered at the G.P.O. as a Newspaper.   TUESDAY, NOVEMBER 11, 1930   One Penny

BUY A POPPY
TO-DAY

ROMANCE OF EMPIRE IN LORD MAYOR'S SHOW

The Lord Mayor's state chariot entering Ludgate Circus.

The new Lord Mayor, Sir William Phené Neal, in his coach at the Guildhall.

A wagon used 100 years ago when British settlers opened up the great North-West.

The National Mark car, in front of which is a figure of Britannia.

A feature of yesterday's Lord Mayor's Show in London was a Pageant of Empire Produce in which were cars illustrating important activities and produce of the Dominions, India and several other parts of the Empire. Four elephants representing India and the " Big Trail " wagon were popular sights. See also page 24.—(" Daily Mirror " photographs.)

THE DAILY MIRROR, Wednesday, November 12, 1930.

TO-DAY'S HISTORIC INDIAN CONFERENCE: P. 2

DailyMirror

THE DAILY PICTURE PAPER WITH THE LARGEST NET SALE

No. 8,419   Registered at the G.P.O. as a Newspaper.   WEDNESDAY, NOVEMBER 12, 1930   One Penny

ARMISTICE NUMBER
PAGES OF SPECIAL PHOTOGRAPHS

"THEY SHALL GROW NOT OLD"

The King and his people share one thought on Twelfth Armistice Day

The thoughts of British men, women and children converged yesterday on the Cenotaph, where the King was present at the already traditional but always new service illustrated above. When, for the twelfth time, life became hushed during two minutes in homage to the 1,000,000 war dead, everyone felt what a poet, Laurence Binyon, has so well expressed. "They shall grow not old, as we that are left grow old: Age shall not weary them, nor the years condemn." See also pages 5, 14, 15 and 28.

MORE THAN £900 PAID IN INSURANCE CLAIMS

MAKE
BOXERS
WORK
By P. J. MOSS

Daily Mirror

THE DAILY PICTURE PAPER WITH THE LARGEST NET SALE

No. 8,424 — Registered at the G.P.O. as a Newspaper. — TUESDAY, NOVEMBER 18, 1930 — One Penny

SPECIAL
EDITION

£658,000 SWEEPSTAKE DRAW

Announcing the names of subscribers and horses drawn at the Mansion House, Dublin, in the Manchester November Handicap sweepstake, for which over £658,000 was subscribed. After the big drum had been revolved a blind boy drew a counterfoil containing a subscriber's name. Simultaneously another blind boy drew a horse's name from the smaller drum. The person named was the drawer of the horse mentioned. This exclusive photograph was brought by "Daily Mirror" aeroplane.

THE DAILY MIRROR, Saturday, November 22, 1930.

NURSE CAVELL: REMARKABLE DISCLOSURES

WIRELESS PROGRAMMES IN FULL ON PAGE 16

DAILY Mirror

THE DAILY PICTURE PAPER WITH THE LARGEST NET SALE

No. 8,428 Registered at the G.P.O. as a Newspaper. SATURDAY, NOVEMBER 22, 1930 One Penny

NEW £500 PUZZLE ON MONDAY

WHO WILL WIN SWEEP FORTUNES TO-DAY?

Mr. James O'Leary, of Cork, and his family, who hold a ticket for Saracen (inset) in the sweepstake for to-day's Manchester November Handicap. Saracen was winner two years ago.

Mrs. Selina Thompson, of Worksop, Nottinghamshire. drew Nestorian.

Mr. G. W. Riley, of Rochdale, Lancs, obtained Redeswood.

Mint Master, a well-backed horse.

Members of a traders' club at Saltley who have a chance with Mint Master.

Who will win the great prizes in the Dublin sweepstake on the Manchester November Handicap, to be run to-day? The first prize will be £204,764, the second £81,905 and the third £40,953. People in many parts of the world have tickets which are worth thousands. Bouverie's selection is Le Voleur.

MASS MILKING ON MERRY-GO-ROUND FOR COWS

Moving slowly in a circle these cows are being milked and groomed at a farm in New Jersey, U.S.A. A platform sixty feet in diameter revolves at the rate of fifteen feet per minute, cleaning and milking 1,680 cows automatically in seven hours. The entire process for each animal takes twelve and a half minutes. The milk is drawn into the sealed glass jars seen above the cows' heads, and thence transferred to a weighing and recording device. Mr. Thomas Edison officially started the machine going yesterday.

THE EDUCATION BILL SHELVED UNTIL 1932

WIRELESS PROGRAMMES ON PAGE 19

DailyMirror

THE DAILY PICTURE PAPER WITH THE LARGEST NET SALE

SPECIAL EDITION

No. 8,431   Registered at the G.P.O. as a Newspaper.   WEDNESDAY, NOVEMBER 26, 1930   One Penny

3,500 LEAVE FLOODED HOMES

LORANG'S SEVEN YEARS

Francis Lorang, who was sentenced at the Old Bailey yesterday to seven years' penal servitude on charges of fraud amounting to £317,000 in connection with the Blue Bird petrol and oil companies of which he was director.

Shopping by means of trestles laid along a street at Viry Chatillon, a suburb of Paris, where 3,500 people had to leave their homes owing to floods.

CHILDREN'S THRILLING EXPERIENCE IN WRECK

Rescuing inhabitants by boat. Alarm is felt throughout Paris and the surrounding districts at the flood menace.—("Daily Mirror" photographs.)

Women and children, passengers of the Highland Hope, who arrived at Southampton yesterday. Mrs. Hinde (light coat) is holding her little daughter Georgina, who asked if she was going for a bathe when being lowered over the wrecked liner's side. See also page 12.

CHILDREN'S XMAS CONTEST: SPLENDID PRIZES

DailyMirror

THE DAILY PICTURE PAPER WITH THE LARGEST NET SALE

No. 8,433   Registered at the G.P.O. as a Newspaper.   FRIDAY, NOVEMBER 28, 1930   One Penny

AMAZING REVELATIONS IN BURNED CAR CASE

Mr. E. Pitt, motor-driver's mate, a witness.

W. Bailey, who with—

—A. T. Brown, stated that he saw the motor-car burning.

Mrs. A. A. Rouse listened to the evidence.

Mr. G. R. Paling, who opened the case.

That the unknown man whose charred body was found in this burned-out car was rendered unconscious, that his clothing was soaked with petrol and set alight are the sensational suggestions made by the prosecution at Northampton, where Alfred Arthur Rouse was again remanded yesterday on a charge of murder. A statement said to have been made by the accused declared that the dead man had asked for a lift and that the fire started when he had been left alone in the car. Rouse is also stated to have declared: "My harem takes me to several places." Counsel said that a mallet on which were human hairs was found near the scene.

£500 FOR DOUBLE-WORDS: NEW PUZZLE CONTEST

WIRELESS PROGRAMMES ON PAGE 23

Daily Mirror

THE DAILY PICTURE PAPER WITH THE LARGEST NET SALE

No. 8,436   Registered at the G.P.O. as a Newspaper.   TUESDAY, DECEMBER 2, 1930   One Penny

MAURICE CHEVALIER'S HITS ON LONDON STAGE

SHOT JAPANESE PREMIER

Maurice Chevalier, the talking-film idol, singing at the Dominion Theatre last night before a packed house.

The young man Tomeo Sagoya, who shot and wounded Mr. O. Hamaguchi, Japanese Prime Minister, at Tokio. The customary straw hood used for prisoners is being put on his head.

With a chorus of English dancers. During his hour on the stage Maurice Chevalier, the most highly-paid actor in the world, sang many songs in French and English, and his best hits were his explanations of the French ones.—(" Daily Mirror " photographs taken by stage lighting.)

Mr. Hamaguchi being carried to the stationmaster's office after he had been shot. He has now practically recovered.

THE DAILY MIRROR, Wednesday, December 3, 1930.

£500 PRIZE IN NEW "DAILY MIRROR" PUZZLE: P. 2

DAILY Mirror

THE DAILY PICTURE PAPER WITH THE LARGEST NET SALE

No. 8,437   Registered at the G.P.O as a Newspaper   WEDNESDAY, DECEMBER 3, 1930   One Penny

GUGNUNC XMAS GIFT FUND

KNIGHTHOODS FOR FRENCH AID TO R101 CREW

M. Couché, to be a Knight Commander of the British Empire.

Mr. Darling, who will receive a letter of commendation.

M. Joly, the Mayor of Beauvais, and—

Commandant Serin (hands raised), to be a Commander of the British Empire, and M. Le Beau, Prefect of the Oise (in overcoat), to become a Knight Commander of the British Empire.

M. L. Le Chat, who will also have a letter of commendation.

M. Henri Huprelle, to have the Meritorious Service Medal.

M. Le Leu, one of the recipients of special souvenirs.

—M. Ballon, Mayor of Allonne, two of the four to receive the C.B.E.

MOTHER WINS FIGHT FOR CHILD

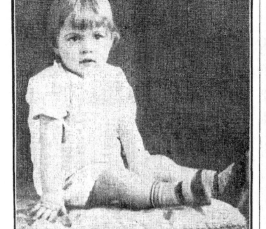

Joan Margaret Carroll, born last year, whose mother has successfully appealed against a judgment refusing to issue a writ for her to have the custody of the child which had been adopted by Protestants. The mother desired the child to be brought up in the Roman Catholic faith into which it had been baptised. The baby is to be handed over to-day.

M. Manceaux with his picture, "Funeral Vigil," which Lord Tyrrell will receive for the Air Council.

Twenty people of Beauvais and Allonne will receive British decorations to-day for their part in helping the survivors and honouring the dead of the airship R 101. Letters of commendation or souvenirs will be given to a number of others. Lord Tyrrell, the British Ambassador in Paris, will make the presentations. Four sacks of gifts have been sent by the British Government for distribution.

NEW SERIES OF CRIME STORIES ON MONDAY

WIRELESS PROGRAMMES ON PAGE 19

DailyMirror

THE DAILY PICTURE PAPER WITH THE LARGEST NET SALE

No. 8,438   Registered at the G.P.O. as a Newspaper.   THURSDAY, DECEMBER 4, 1930   One Penny

NEW £500 PUZZLE TO-DAY

PRINCESS IN FANCY DRESS

DEATH DIARY

Dr. Hugh Lonsdale Hands, of Brighton, recorded his sensations after taking a fatal dose of poison. Extracts from his last letters were read at the inquest yesterday, when a verdict of Suicide while of unsound mind was recorded. He wrote: "Feeling very happy. First time ever felt without worry. Death is lovely."

FIGHT FOR CHILD SEQUEL

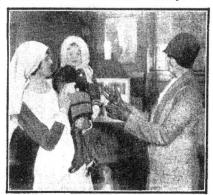

Joan Margaret Carroll, whose mother, in a long legal battle, obtained her return from a society that she might be brought up a Roman Catholic, being handed yesterday to Mrs. A. P. Woods, who has been nominated to take care of the child for five years.

The Duchess of York with Princess Elizabeth, dressed as a fairy, leaving Londonderry House yesterday after Lady Mary Stewart's birthday party. It was the first time that the Princess, who was four years old in April, had been to a fancy dress party. See also page 12.—("Daily Mirror" photograph.)

119

BEGIN THE MASTER MYSTERIES ON MONDAY

WIRELESS PROGRAMMES ON PAGE 17

DailyMirror

THE DAILY PICTURE PAPER WITH THE LARGEST NET SALE

SPECIAL EDITION

No. 8,440   Registered at the G.P.O. as a Newspaper.   SATURDAY, DECEMBER 6, 1930   One Penny

HONOUR FOR AGED SCIENTIST

Dr. Griffith Evans, the eminent scientist, upon whom Bangor, Carnarvonshire, Council have decided to confer the freedom of the city. He is ninety-six years of age and bedridden.

LL.G. ON "SETS OF FOOTLERS"

Mr. Lloyd George addressing the meeting of the Liberal Candidates' Association at the National Liberal Club yesterday morning. Explaining why he could see no wisdom in turning the Government out to let in the Conservatives, he said: "A country is never saved by swopping one set of footlers for another."

'CHASER LANDS ON ITS NOSE

Two phases of the heavy fall of Solomon's Choice two fences from home in the Effingham Handicap 'Chase at Sandown Park yesterday. P. Prendergast was the jockey.—("Daily Mirror.")

SUBSIDY MOVE

Mr. R. M. Ford, of Albertgate, who applied in the Chancery Division yesterday for an injunction to restrain the Postmaster - General from handing over £17,500 to the B.B.C. This followed the Government's decision to subsidise opera.

'MEDICAL LIES'

The late Dr. Hugh Lonsdale Hands, of Brighton, who left a remarkable message for the Press, revealed yesterday. "The medical profession is all wrong," it says. "It is all money: lies: massage: bedside manner: nursing homes."

WHO WAS GUILTY? NEW FEATURE ON PAGE 15

WIRELESS PROGRAMMES ON PAGE 17

DailyMirror

THE DAILY PICTURE PAPER WITH THE LARGEST NET SALE

No. 8,441   Registered at the G.P.O. as a Newspaper.   MONDAY, DECEMBER 8, 1930   One Penny

SPECIAL EDITION

HERO OF BELGIAN DEATH FOG | NEW BERET

Dr. Gendelin, who worked unceasingly for twenty-four hours in the thick fog that terrorised the valley of the Meuse in Belgium. Right, a house at Engis in which a whole family of six died from the effects of the fog. More deaths have occurred since it lifted.

MAN FOUND DEAD WITH HEAD BATTERED

Mr. Charles Benfold. He was thirty-seven.

A charming interpretation of the modern beret made in black felt and velour. Reslaw.—(" Daily Mirror " photograph.)

WOMAN'S FLIGHT ACROSS TWO CONTINENTS

The house in Oliver-street, South Moor, Co. Durham, where Charles Benfold was found dead with his head badly battered. An inquest will be held to-day. His wife made the discovery.

The Hon. Mrs. Victor Bruce welcomed at Osaka at the conclusion of her flight from England to Japan, the first ever to have been accomplished. Huge crowds greeted her.

"HIS LAST PERFORMANCE": SOLUTION ON P. 18

WIRELESS PROGRAMMES ON PAGE 19

DailyMirror

THE DAILY PICTURE PAPER WITH THE LARGEST NET SALE

SPECIAL EDITION

No. 8,447   Registered at the G.P.O. as a Newspaper.   MONDAY, DECEMBER 15, 1930   One Penny

RIOTING AND REVOLT IN TROUBLED SPAIN

A tramcar overturned during recent riots in Valencia, Spain. Two leaders of the revolt recently suppressed at the military stronghold of Jaca were executed yesterday after being sentenced to death by court-martial.

SHOT IN GAME

Leonard James Hibbert, aged ten, of Bushey, Herts, who was accidentally shot in the back while playing at soldiers with a friend. He died later.

MARQUIS ILL

The Marquis of Salisbury, who is suffering from the effects of overwork and has been ordered a complete rest. He is sixty-nine years of age.—("Daily Mirror")

Arresting a rioter. Two strikers were killed and a policeman shot and seriously injured.

HELP THE GUGNUNC CHRISTMAS FUND NOW

WIRELESS PROGRAMMES ON PAGE 17

DailyMirror

THE DAILY PICTURE PAPER WITH THE LARGEST NET SALE

No. 8,451 Registered at the G.P.O. as a Newspaper. FRIDAY, DECEMBER 19, 1930 One Penny

SPECIAL EDITION

FIASCO OF £1,750,000 WATERWORKS

BOY KILLED IN A FACTORY LIFT

Alfred Reiss, aged eighteen, who was killed in a lift at a toy factory where he was employed. He is stated to have remarked, " I have only got to die once," before he jumped into the lift. He lived in Stepney Green.

The lower end of the Broomhead Reservoir, part of the great Ewden Valley waterworks scheme which cost Sheffield £1,750,000 and has proved a fiasco as a geological defect prevents the water flowing. (Inset) Mr. Arthur Greenwood, Socialist Minister of Health in 1929, who inaugurated the scheme.

PEER'S COUSIN SHOT DEAD ON CASTLE ESTATE

EARL'S DAUGHTER MARRIED

Saltwood Castle, Hythe, Kent, in the grounds of which Mr. Reginald Lawson (inset), who is a cousin of Lord Burnham, was found shot dead. It is believed that the trigger of his gun became entangled in barbed wire.

Mr. Reginald Manningham-Buller and his bride, Lady Mary Lindsay, daughter of the Earl and Countess of Crawford, after their marriage yesterday at St. Margaret's, Westminster. The Archbishop of Canterbury officiated.

DOUBLE-WORDS THE BEST XMAS PUZZLE:

ORDER TO-DAY

DailyMirror

THE DAILY PICTURE PAPER WITH THE LARGEST NET SALE

SPECIAL EDITION

No. 8,452   Registered at the G.P.O. as a Newspaper.   SATURDAY, DECEMBER 20, 1930   One Penny

PARALYTIC'S MURDER TRIAL   WED ON FRIDAY

George Small lying prone on a couch with guards beside him during his trial at King's County Court, Brooklyn, United States, on a charge of murder. The accused man is completely paralysed below the waist by a bullet which was fired by a policeman and has lodged in his spine.

Mr. John Holt Wilson and his bride, Roberta Lady Ossulston, after marriage at Chelsea register office yesterday. The bride wore green orchids for this Friday wedding.

"PERFECT BOY" PRIZE

S. E. Raymond, a pupil of Fortescue House School, Twickenham, Middlesex, has won the prize given by the Queen to the boy who best carries out the motto "Be Good and Do Good." He is to go into Civil Service.

COMMISSIONER INSPECTS TRAFFIC POLICE

Colonel Laurie adjusting the white armlet of one of the 500 Metropolitan policemen who are to go on traffic patrol duty. They were inspected by Vice-Admiral Sir C. W. R. Royds, Acting Commissioner at Scotland Yard.—("Daily Mirror.")

CRASH IN SEA

Flight-Lieutenant J. Boothman, one of the high-speed flying team of pilots at Felixstowe, was badly bruised when his machine, one of the Schneider Trophy type, overturned at sea yesterday.

THE DAILY MIRROR, Tuesday, December 23, 1930.

MANY INSURANCE CLAIMS PAID: REGISTER NOW

WIRELESS PROGRAMMES ON PAGE 17

Daily Mirror

THE DAILY PICTURE PAPER WITH THE LARGEST NET SALE

No. 8,454 — Registered at the G.P.O. as a Newspaper. — TUESDAY, DECEMBER 23, 1930 — One Penny

£100 CROSSWORD PUZZLE

HAIR-RAISING AERIAL ACT IN OLYMPIA CIRCUS

Father Christmas (Whimsical Walker) talking to Mr. Ramsay MacDonald at the opening performance

Watching the thrilling tight-rope act performed by the Wallendas high above the great circus ring.

A Shetland pony bowing during Captain Bertram Mills's circus at Olympia. Every kind of circus entertainment is provided, and the Wallendas' hair-raising aerial turn is the big feat of the show.

The Earl of Lonsdale giving bouquets during the show, which the Lord Mayor, Sir Phené Neal, opened.

125

BEGIN "FALLING STAR" TO-DAY ON PAGE 13

WIRELESS PROGRAMMES ON PAGE 17

DailyMirror

THE DAILY PICTURE PAPER WITH THE LARGEST NET SALE

No. 8,456   Registered at the G.P.O. as a Newspaper.   SATURDAY, DECEMBER 27, 1930   One Penny

£500 DOUBLE WORDS PUZZLE

RIDER'S STEEPLECHASE SPILL

OFFICIAL MURDERED IN BURMESE RIOT

Remarkable "Daily Mirror" photograph of Captain R. E. Sassoon being thrown by Mrs. N. Colls's Middle Ages during the Amateurs' Handicap Steeplechase at Kempton Park yesterday. Sir Shaun won.

Mr. H. V. W. Fields-Clarke, a Government engineer, who was murdered during a serious outbreak in the Tharrawaddy and Insein districts in Burma. The police were repulsed by rioters at one time and troops are being rushed to the scene.

ROMANCE OF THE STAGE

Miss Ursula Jeans, whose engagement to Mr. Robin Irvine (inset) is announced. She is now playing in "The First Mrs. Fraser" and her fiance is appearing in "Caviare."

PRINCE ARTHUR CARVES HOSPITAL TURKEY

Prince Arthur of Connaught wearing an apron to cut the first slice off the turkey in the presence of Princess Arthur at the Middlesex Hospital. He is chairman of the hospital,— ("Daily Mirror" photograph.)

A DICTATOR

Prince Louis of Monaco, who after a week of political tension, has suspended the National and Communal Councils of the Principality, making himself absolute dictator.

Made in the USA
Coppell, TX
04 January 2022

70911271R00070